PRAISE FOR *FIN*

I thank God for *Finding Quiet*. Here J. P. Moreland, a first-rate philosopher, provides us with wise and deeply personal insights into anxiety and depression. In doing so, he gives us a most useful understanding of the functioning of the human soul. I highly recommend *Finding Quiet*.

RICHARD J. FOSTER, author of *Celebration of Discipline*

Finding Quiet is a remarkable book. I am grateful that J. P. Moreland researched the topic of anxiety and depression so deeply and then shared his findings through his own story. His personal vulnerability is both encouraging and convicting. Whether you wrestle with anxiety and depression yourself or know someone who does, this book is full of wisdom and practical steps that make it an invaluable resource.

SEAN MCDOWELL, Biola University professor,
speaker, author

Anxiety and depression are unfortunately far too common and can be highly severe, even life-threatening. J. P. Moreland's book is a personal, vulnerable, and instructive guide from his own narrative to what has helped him and to what can make a difference to the reader. His biblical references are especially enlightening. Highly recommended.

DR. JOHN TOWNSEND, *New York Times* bestselling
author of *Boundaries* and founder of the Townsend
Institute for Leadership and Counseling

Here's a masterpiece of scholarship, transparency, compassion, and profound guidance for all who struggle with anxiety or depression. My friend J. P. Moreland courageously opens his life so you can move toward healing and hope. This book will be a blessed breakthrough for countless readers!

LEE STROBEL, *New York Times* bestselling author

J. P. Moreland is not only a leading philosopher; he's also a man who has seen sore affliction due to stress and anxiety. In light of his candid account of his recovery from two nervous breakdowns, J. P. explains how broken people can find peace and wholeness through counseling, meditation, prayer, and medication. As a philosopher, he makes a strong case for his positions. I found especially helpful his argument for Christians taking medications that help with depression and anxiety. But he is more than philosophical; he's pastoral. He uses his experience and research to help mend wounded people. In this, he is like Jesus, who was given "a well-instructed tongue to know the word that sustains the weary" (Isaiah 50:4). This book will help me find some of the joy and serenity I've lost in recent years.

DOUGLAS GROOTHUIS, professor of philosophy at
Denver Seminary and author of *Walking through Twilight:
A Wife's Illness—A Philosopher's Lament*

Don't be fooled by the title. *Finding Quiet* doesn't minimize depression one bit or offer superficial solutions. Its well-researched ideas combine depth and practicality, providing a path to survive—even thrive—in living in the fullness of God.

JAN JOHNSON, author of *When the Soul Listens* and
coauthor of *Renovation of the Heart in Daily Practice*

Finding Quiet is a wide-ranging and remarkably helpful analysis of the causes and solutions for anxiety and depression. It draws on the findings of modern psychology, the timeless truths of the Bible, and the author's own personal struggle with anxiety to provide a multifaceted remedy that will give readers genuine hope for dealing with their own anxiety and depression or helping others who face these challenges.

WAYNE GRUDEM, research professor of theology
and biblical studies at Phoenix Seminary

In his Sermon on the Mount, Jesus repeatedly enjoins us not to be anxious (Matthew 6:25–34). The apostle Paul reinforces this admonition when he writes, "Do not be anxious about anything" (Philippians 4:6). But *how*? Many of us feel powerless to banish anxiety from our lives. It just happens. And sometimes we find that the more we try to deal with it, the more anxiety we feel precisely because we cannot overcome it. In this practical, insightful, and immensely helpful book, J. P. Moreland imparts the wisdom he has acquired in his years of personal struggle with anxiety—an integrative wisdom coming from the fields of neuroscience, psychology, psychiatry, medicine, and philosophy. He combines this with a set of biblical spiritual practices that make a profound difference in the quality of one's life. If you struggle with anxiety, this book will give you hope.

CLINTON E. ARNOLD, dean and professor of
New Testament at Talbot School of Theology
(Biola University)

Finding Quiet is a deeply moving, honest, and helpful resource. J. P. Moreland writes from his heart and out of his personal experiences about his own pathway back from anxiety and depression to peace and joy. Make no mistake, this philosopher is also a soulologist who has written a book that is holistic, practical, and a must-read for Christians who are experiencing anxiety and depression. Here you will find an excellent complement to the process of Christian counseling and psychotherapy.

> GARY W. MOON, executive director of the Martin Institute
> for Christianity and Culture and Dallas Willard Center,
> Westmont College, and author of *Becoming Dallas Willard:
> The Formation of a Philosopher, Teacher, and Christ Follower*

An extremely vulnerable, raw, yet well-researched, biblical approach to practically replacing anxiety with the joy and peace God promises. Any Christ-follower who wants to grow in the experience of peace and joy will benefit from the spiritual formation path this book lays out.

> JOHN BURKE, pastor and *New York Times* bestselling
> author of *Imagine Heaven* and *No Perfect People Allowed*

FINDING QUIET

My Story of Overcoming Anxiety and the Practices That Brought Peace

J. P. MORELAND

CONTENTS

Preface

The book you hold in your hands is an honest revelation of my own struggles with anxiety and depression, along with a selection of the significant spiritual, physical, and psychological ideas and practices that have helped me most. I am not a licensed therapist, and this book is not meant to be a substitute for professional psychological or psychiatric help. Rather, my intent is to come alongside you, my reader, as a fellow sufferer and to share my experiences and some ideas and practices that may be fresh and new to you. These ideas and practices have helped many, but my book is my own story, and everyone's experiences are unique. There is much to learn about dealing with anxiety and depression; may this book encourage you as you seek to meet your own mental health needs.

A clinical psychologist read an earlier draft of the manuscript, and I incorporated his suggestions. Moreover, some of my thinking in this book reflects not just my training in seminary in pastoral counseling, which has been part of my ministry for more than forty years, but also the lessons I've learned over the years from close friends who are therapists.

If you suffer from anxiety or depression or another mental health issue, please know that I am a fellow sufferer, and I want you to improve. I pray you will find hope and help in the pages to follow.

I am indebted to Hope Moreland, Bill Roth, Becky Heatley, and Jim Duncan for reading an early draft of this book and providing me with helpful feedback.

Introduction

My Descent(s) into an Abyss of Anxiety/ Depression

MAY 24, 2003, 2:30 A.M. On Friday afternoon, May 23, 2003, I had attended Biola University's graduation ceremony. School was finally over, and I was looking forward to a nine-month sabbatical to write, rest, be with my family, and do some traveling and speaking. Little did I know that I was about to face the worst seven months of my life.

I am not a light sleeper, but at 2:30 in the morning of May 24, I awoke dripping wet with sweat, my heart pounding through my chest, and my body filled with electricity and adrenaline. It was as though I sensed a large tiger in the house, and I went from room to room to see if something was wrong. The previous nine-month school year had been the most stressful time in my life, at least since early childhood. Yet something was happening to me that I had never encountered before and of which I had no understanding. Unknown to me, I was having a severe panic attack.

My wife, Hope, woke up to ask what was wrong, and all I could tell her was that I was shaking, that electricity was running from the back of my head to my chest, and that I was very afraid but did not know of what. I decided to take a walk around our block, and I did so until the sun came up. That weekend I must have walked around our block a hundred times. Two specific thoughts were anxiety-producing for me, and I could not get them out of my mind. One thought was about a critic of me and my work who was spreading lies about my character. Eventually, he was identified and exposed by others, but I did not know this would happen. All I could think about were his attacks and the fact that my life's work would be undone. The second thought was that I was going to lose my job as a professor because of these false attacks, which would leave my family and me destitute. When you are anxious, you don't always think rationally, yet these thoughts seemed very, very real and dangerous to me.

As I walked all weekend, I battled with those thoughts, trying to find some distance and relief from them. On Monday morning, I had (of all things) jury duty. I was not called to serve, but for seven hours that day, I lay on the floor in the back of the jury-pool room and tried to read one of Dallas Willard's books. By midafternoon, I had fallen apart. I was in the midst of the most frightening, fragmenting battle for my sanity I had ever known.

MY BACKGROUND. To provide some context, let's flash back to my childhood. As far as anxiety and depression are concerned, by the time I was seven years old, I already had two strikes against me: genetic ancestry and early childhood. I was born with a clear genetic predisposition to anxiety from my mother's side of the family. My maternal grandfather was a nervous wreck. I have memories of him visiting us and not being able to stay seated or keep from bouncing his legs and fidgeting with his fingers. He was very anxious, and when any of us would get near him, we couldn't help unintentionally internalizing his anxiety. My mother lived in fear and anxiety on a daily basis, as did her sister and brother. She and her sister were taking valium for the last twenty years of their lives, and my uncle self-medicated by drinking. And I have other relatives on my mother's side who have been on antidepressant or anxiety medication for years. I have two daughters. One looks like me and my mother, and the other looks like my wife and my biological father. Guess what—the former has my anxiety and is on medications and in counseling, while the other daughter does not need medication. My genetic predisposition is just that—a predisposition I inherited that does not determine my behavior, but it does make getting anxious a lot easier for me than for those without the predisposition, all things being equal.

My early childhood was traumatic. I learned how to worry by watching and absorbing my mother's constant fretting. After I got married and my mother was older, when my family and I went back to the Kansas City area to visit her and my stepfather—I kid you not—each door of their house had at least six locks on it, and they lived in a safe neighborhood. My mother looked at the world through the eyes of fear, and as I explore in the next chapter, anxiety is partly a learned habit, and I learned from the best!

Besides that, my father contracted terminal cancer of the liver when I was seven months in the womb. When I was six weeks old, my parents left me at my grandparents' home, and my mother took Dad to Jefferson City, where a radical surgeon (someone who would perform a risky, untested surgery on a patient who had no alternative; there was no guarantee the surgery would work) worked on my father and removed the cancer, or so we thought. Eventually, the cancer came back, and Dad died when I was seven years old. I have vivid memories of his eyes being yellow and of him reaching for a glass of orange juice, only to miss the glass and spill everything on the floor. I asked my mother, "Daddy is dying, isn't he?" but she dismissed the question. I was not allowed to grieve but was constantly distracted with new toys and was not permitted to go to his funeral after he died. My father never found himself. He always wanted to be a coach, but being a salesman was the only way he could provide adequately for the family. He hated his job and was discouraged most of the time. From the time of the radical surgery until his death in 1955, he and my mother were also on constant alert for the cancer to return. The job and the cancer was more than he could take. He was a good man, but a depressed one.

Five years later, when I was in seventh grade, my mom remarried. My stepfather, Larry, was a good and decent man, but he did not know how to relate to a son (though he tried), and he did not know how to express or speak about emotions. I left for college in 1966 with a lot of fear about being able to handle it. I also had a hole in my heart that could only be filled by finding real meaning in life. Fortunately, I found Jesus there in 1968 through Campus Crusade for Christ, and I joined the Crusade staff for five years.

After that, I went to Dallas Seminary, married my precious wife, Hope, halfway through seminary in 1977, and moved to San Bernardino, California, where we lived from 1979 to 1984. During that time, I taught at Crusade's seminary; my wife gave birth to our two precious daughters—Ashley and Allison (now married, in their mid-thirties, and with five children); and I did an MA and a PhD in philosophy under Dallas Willard. We moved a few times before settling in Yorba Linda, California, in 1990, and I have taught philosophy at Biola University ever since.

Throughout these years, I was anxious and depressed from time to time, but not in any way that made me unable to function. That is, until 2:30 a.m. on May 24, 2003, when all hell broke loose.

BACK TO 2003. For seven months, I experienced daily panic attacks and felt intense anxiety except when sleeping. I could not see the world as it really is. I spent a lot of time for the first month or so lying on the couch because I did not have the energy to get up. I was afraid of irrational things. I was in fear every time I checked my email, and my heart would start pounding every time the phone rang. I could not drive on the freeway—it was too much stimulation. I could not attend my grandchildren's soccer games, and for about six weeks, I could not have them in my home.

I wanted to be left alone, so I often curled up in a ball and worried about everything. I can remember wanting desperately to get out of my own skin, but I was stuck in it. I never seriously contemplated suicide, but many times I asked God to kill me in an automobile accident or in some other way. I thought my whole life had been a waste, and I saw no purpose for living. I wanted to die so the pain would go away.

I started weekly therapy with a good Christian therapist, and I went to our primary care physician, who prescribed an antidepressant medication. This was a good decision, but it can be a complicated affair choosing to go on medication and which caregivers to consult about it. In my case, the dosage prescribed by my primary care doctor didn't help. Two months later, a friend said I should see a psychiatrist, since they are specialists in medications and brain chemistry. Sometimes the cost of seeing a psychiatrist is prohibitive or one may not be accessible, and there are times when one's primary care team may offer better guidance on medications than a psychiatrist. But in my case, I needed to try something else. My psychiatrist significantly adjusted my dosage. The medication, my therapy, my friends, and lots of Bible reading and prayer helped, and the day after Christmas, my anxiety and depression lifted. I was "well," but the whole experience left me a broken man and a different person. It had been a terrifying seven months. I continued in therapy and stayed on medication while easing back into my job, still fearful of a relapse. I felt relatively normal for the next ten years until May 11, 2013.

MAY 11, 2013. Since I had been feeling better for so long, I foolishly took on far too much work for the school year of

2012–2013. On top of that I worked with my psychiatrist to lower my dosage to a smaller amount. I did not know it, but I was a sitting duck for a relapse. It happened late in the afternoon on May 11, 2013. When you are prone to anxiety, stress is enemy number one—*But not for me*, I thought. After all, I was a distinguished professor and Christian "leader," whatever that means. Surely all this panic attack business was behind me. I think the weekly activities of university teaching helped suppress any growing anxiety. But with just one week left in the spring semester, having just presented a philosophical paper at a high-level academic conference, I walked to my car to go home—and boom! Seemingly out of nowhere, I was hit with a relapse of panic, terrorizing fear, and high-level anxiety. I can remember thinking, *Please, God, not again! I can't take another period of anxiety like I did in 2003.* But I did. This time, the gruesome period of anxiety and depression lasted five months.

I immediately tried to slow down, but when things were quiet and I had nothing to do, my mind found fears on which to obsess. I got back on a higher dosage of antidepressant medication and started back into therapy. I was in serious trouble all summer and dreaded the day the fall semester was going to start.

I tried to teach my classes but was horrified by being in the classroom. I got to the point where I would go to the empty classroom in which I was about to teach an hour before class, walk around the room, stand at the lectern, and try to convince myself that there was nothing to be afraid of. But it didn't work. Two weeks into the semester, I had to drop out and stop teaching. I thank God that my department chair and dean were able to find people to cover for me so the classes could continue. I was embarrassed and discouraged, and I didn't know who I was.

The low point came in early October when I joined a two-week anxiety-depression group at a nearby hospital. I am an advocate of group therapy, and my therapist friends value it. But for some reason or other, I wasn't into it this time. My heart and mind were elsewhere. I went to the hospital each day from 8 a.m. until 4 p.m. There were about twenty other people in the group, most of whom were very different from me and I couldn't relate to them. I felt like a fish out of water.

One afternoon it hit me—at the very time I was in my group of sad people who looked like they were at the end of their lives (most had been in the group for months), my classes were being taught by other people and Biola was chugging along without me. From my anxiety-ridden, skewed perspective, the contrast between my group and my life at Biola was so stark that I simply started crying and could not stop. I was at rock bottom again.

After the two-week group ended, I went home, and a few days later, God spoke to me. He told me he never wanted this to happen to me again, and while he would be with me, I needed to see the future weeks and months as a learning pilgrimage. I needed to learn all I could about anxiety and depression and begin to practice daily what I learned. So from mid-October until mid-January, I read—no, devoured—at least forty books, both secular and Christian, on the psychology of anxiety and on formative spiritual principles. I learned a ton and took detailed notes on the most helpful points.

This approach might not have worked for everyone. All I can say is what I learned and began to practice changed me in a way that I intuitively knew was different. I was becoming a different person, and my family and friends noticed the difference. The chapters to follow are a condensation of the very best and most helpful things I discovered. I know for a fact they worked in my life. How do I know?

AUGUST 3, 2015—THE START OF A MEDICAL NIGHT-MARE. In June 2015, my routine blood work showed that my PSA was extremely high. My doctor referred me to a urologist, who did a biopsy on my prostate gland and told me that half of it was filled with cancer. Thankfully, none had penetrated the prostate wall, so on August 3, I had a radical prostatectomy to remove my prostate gland. The surgery took five hours, and I needed two blood transfusions during the operation.

For the next two years, I was to get a PSA blood test every three months to check on how things were going. After such a surgery, one's PSA should stay below .05. If it gets to .21, that is a good indicator that surgery did not get all the cancer and that radiation would be needed. My readings (two to three months apart) were .03, .04, .29, .38, .31, .39, and .51. When my PSA reached 1.5, my urologist said I was having a relapse of cancer, so in the fall of 2017, I received thirty-nine radiation treatments along with Lupron injections that help to starve the prostate cancer cells. As I write this, it will take about a year before I will know if I'm prostate cancer-free.

Then in late January 2014, I started to get out of breath after doing simple activities like bringing in a small bag of groceries. After a general blood test, my doctor told me my iron levels were lower than any patient he had seen in twenty years. He almost sent me to the hospital for a blood transfusion. He told me it had to be due to internal bleeding, so I had a colonoscopy in March, and a very large tumor was discovered in my cecum (the area at the junction of the small and large intestines). Another five-hour surgery removed a massive tumor that involved thirty-one lymph nodes. Only one node was cancerous, but it had penetrated my colon wall, and I would need to have six to seven months of chemotherapy. Every other week, I'd get infused with three different cancer-killing drugs for about six hours at the cancer center. Then I wore a pump for forty-eight hours that was inserted into a port from my chest to my heart, and it continued to pump chemo into me.

My health situation deteriorated further. During a routine visit with my dermatologist, the doctor cut out a strange-looking lesion on the back of my left arm. None of the labs could diagnose it, so they sent it to Harvard and to UCLA, which came up with the same diagnosis: I had a very rare skin cancer (it usually occurs around the eyes, and only 120 cases have been reported in the US in other areas of the body) called a sebaceous carcinoma that was caused by a rare disease known as Muir-Torre syndrome, a form of Lynch syndrome. None of my doctors had heard of it. It is a rare, highly malignant, life-threatening cancer. If it metastasizes, it is virtually a death sentence.

I didn't know how long the lesion had been there—three months or three years. Surgery was scheduled immediately, and I now have an eight-inch scar on the back of my arm and a large scar under my arm.

I also got a squamous cell carcinoma on my forehead. It was deep, and while I have a hole in my head (as many have told me for years), I now required another surgery. The wound was kept open, and I wore a large bandage on my forehead for two and a half months.

What's the point of all this? During a two-year period, I contracted four cancers, had four inpatient surgeries and one outpatient surgery, and was on chemotherapy for seven months. Yet I was the happiest, calmest, and most peaceful I had been in years! I had virtually no anxiety at all. I am not exaggerating. My close friends, my wife, and my daughters regularly commented they couldn't believe how peaceful and happy I was throughout it all. The reason was that for about two years, I had been practicing the things I'd discovered.

My deepest hope and prayer is that what I share in the pages to follow will give you hope and confidence and will prompt your own healing journey. Remember, if you or a loved one struggles with anxiety or depression, I am one of you. I know exactly what it feels like, and I know the frustration in your heart and the longing to get better. So I offer what follows with the hope that what encouraged and helped me may also encourage and help you. May God make it so. As a transition to the book's first chapter, I offer you a word of encouragement. Chapter 1 may be a bit difficult for some readers in that it is somewhat theologically heavy. Some may need to read it twice before proceeding to chapter 2. But please read it carefully, because it provides a spiritual framework within which to better understand mental health.

One final point: While anxiety and depression are different, one can cause the other, and they often occur together. And treatments for one are often effective for the other. As psychologist Deborah Glasofer notes, "Do not despair if you think you suffer from separate, co-occurring anxiety and mood symptoms . . . There is an overlap in effective psychotherapies for these problems; similarly, a group of medications known as selective serotonin reuptake inhibitors (SSRIs) are among those that have been shown to be helpful with both anxiety and depression."[1]

In what follows, I will often speak of anxiety alone. This is for the sake of convenience, and while I have suffered from both anxiety and depression, I am more familiar with the former. But you may understand that much of what I learned about anxiety applies equally to depression.

Chapter 1

HUMAN PERSONS AND A HOLISTIC APPROACH FOR DEFEATING ANXIETY/DEPRESSION

Extrabiblical Knowledge

It was a very hot Southern California afternoon in August 2007, but thank the Lord, I was preaching in a nicely air-conditioned church with about one thousand people in attendance. The pastor was gone on vacation to Europe. I had preached at this church four times previously, and I was enjoying the morning immensely. While making a point in my message, I rather offhandedly mentioned that I was on an antidepressant, and I urged people who were struggling with anxiety/depression to check out this avenue of help. Well, my point was like teeing off a golf ball in the shower: It quickly ricocheted right back at me! As soon as the service ended, two elders rushed me into a back room and told me in no uncertain terms that their church did not believe in such medications. I was never invited back.

The disciplines of psychiatry and psychology are widely rejected by evangelicals. As one Christian leader put it, "True psychology ('the study of the soul') can be done only by Christians, since only Christians have the resources for the understanding and the transformation of the soul. Since the secular discipline of psychology is based on godless assumptions and evolutionary foundations, it is capable of dealing with people only superficially and only on the temporal level . . . Scripture is the manual for all 'soul work.'"[1]

In stark contrast to this approach, consider the words of

John Wesley: "To imagine none can teach you but those who are themselves saved from sin, is a very great and dangerous mistake. Give not place to it for a moment."[2] In valuing extrabiblical knowledge, our brothers and sisters throughout church history were merely following common sense and Scripture itself.

Repeatedly, Scripture acknowledges the wisdom of cultures outside Israel—for example, Egypt (Isaiah 19:11–13), the Edomites (Jeremiah 49:7), the Phoenicians (Zechariah 9:2), and many, many others. The remarkable achievements produced by human wisdom are acknowledged in Job 28:1–11. The wisdom of Solomon is compared to that of "all the people of the east" and "all the wisdom of Egypt" to show that it surpassed that of people with a longstanding, well-deserved reputation for wisdom (1 Kings 4:29–34). Paul approvingly quotes pagan philosophers (Acts 17:28), and Jude cites the noncanonical book Assumption of Moses in Jude 9. The book of Proverbs is filled with examples in which knowledge, even moral and spiritual knowledge, can be gained from studying things (for example, ants) in the natural world. Once Jesus taught that we should know we are to love our enemies, not on the basis of an Old Testament text, but from careful reflection on how the sun and rain behave (Matthew 5:44–45). We can and must cultivate a Christian approach to anxiety and depression, but in that tilling we may also include the study of extrabiblical knowledge that supplements and does not contradict Scripture.

I believe naysayers make two mistakes: (1) They have seen abuses of "all truth is God's truth" and have thrown the baby out with the bathwater, and (2) they fail to see the implications of a biblical view of the human person for developing and sustaining mental health. Regarding the first mistake, "all truth is God's truth" has sometimes been used as a slogan to justify revising the Bible to fit a claim to truth that is not within a legitimate interpretation of Scripture. When it comes to psychology, a believer must always check what one hears against biblical teaching and the wisdom of a group of mature believers. But the abuse of something does not determine its legitimate use. Indeed, "all truth is God's truth" has been horribly abused, but with proper caution, there is so much good, helpful, and true information from the field of psychology and psychiatry that we would be foolish not to appropriate it.

Regarding the second mistake, I believe the naysayers have a faulty, or at least an underdeveloped, view of the Bible's teaching about the functional, holistic nature of human beings. Let me explain.

HEALING ANXIETY/DEPRESSION AND THE HUMAN PERSON

Several months ago, my wife and I attended a spiritual formation class at our church. The speaker mentioned the "self" and the "ego" as part of her lecture. A class member's hand shot up: "How does the self or ego relate to the soul and spirit?" An older gentleman immediately followed with a comment: "I've been a Christian for thirty years, and I have no idea what a soul is. No one has ever taught on the subject."

As Dallas Willard said in many of his lectures and writings, without an understanding of the soul and the body and their relationship to each other, it is impossible to think deeply and helpfully about spiritual formation and growing as a disciple of Jesus, and that includes ways to defeat anxiety.[3] For example, according to Willard, if one does not understand the deep connections between the brain and emotions, one will most likely address anxiety as a purely spiritual or psychological issue, leaving out entirely the importance of factoring in issues involving the brain. It is precisely these topics and more that I will address in this chapter.

THE HUMAN SOUL

Put very simply, the soul is an immaterial substance or thing that contains consciousness and animates/enlivens the body.[4] Consciousness is what we are aware of when we intro-spect. It consists in sensations (pain, the taste of a lemon), thoughts, beliefs, desires, memories, acts of free choice, and so on. As I will show later in the chapter, these are in the soul, not the brain.

Further, the soul is fully present at each point of the body. In this way, the soul is to the body as God is to space—entirely present at each point. This is part of what it means to say that the soul animates, makes alive, makes sentient the body. That's why you don't lose, say, 10 percent of your soul if your arm is cut off, or 50 percent of your soul when half of your brain is removed in surgery.

This is important to know because many of our emotions

and sensations, including anxiety, reside in certain parts of our bodies—we feel the anxiety there—because our soul is at those places and is the literal container of the emotions or sensations. And as we will see, gaining victory over anxiety includes cultivating the ability of noticing: being aware of the different feelings/sensations and their locations in the embodied soul.

Finally, the soul contains what is called faculties. At any given time, the soul has a number of capacities or abilities that are not currently being actualized or used. To understand this, consider an acorn. The acorn has certain actual characteristics or states—a specific size or color. It also has a number of capacities or potentialities that could become actual if certain things happen. For example, the acorn has the capacity to grow a root system or change into the shape of a tree.

Likewise, the soul has capacities. I have the ability to see color, think about math, or desire ice cream even when I am asleep and not in the actual states just mentioned. The adult human soul has literally thousands of capacities within its structure. But the soul is not just a scrambled collection of isolated, discrete, randomly related internal capacities. Rather, the various capacities within the soul fall into natural groupings called faculties of the soul.

In order to grab hold of this, think for a moment about this list of capacities: the ability to see red, see orange, hear a dog bark, hear a tune, think about math, think about God, desire lunch, desire a family. The ability to see red is more closely related to the ability to see orange than it is to the ability to think about math. We express this insight by saying that the abilities to see red or orange are parts of the same faculty—the faculty of sight. The ability to think about math is a capacity within the thinking faculty—the mind. In general, a faculty is a compartment of the soul that contains a naturally resembling family of related capacities.

We are now in a position to map out the soul in more detail. All the soul's capacities to see are part of the faculty of sight. If my eyeballs are defective, then my soul's faculty of sight will be inoperative, just as a driver cannot get to work in his or her car if the spark plugs are broken. Likewise, if my eyeballs work but my soul is inattentive, say, I am daydreaming, then I won't see what is before me either.

The soul also contains faculties of smell, touch, taste, and hearing. Taken together, these five are called sensory faculties of the soul. The will is a faculty of the soul that contains my capacities to choose. The emotional faculty of the soul contains one's abilities to experience fear, love, and so forth.

Two additional faculties of the soul are of crucial importance. The *mind* is that faculty of the soul that contains thoughts and beliefs, along with the relevant abilities to reason with them. It is with my mind that I think, and my mind contains my beliefs. However, if my brain is damaged, it will affect my ability to think, recall memories, and so on.

The *spirit* is that faculty of the soul through which the person relates to God (Psalm 51:10; Romans 8:16; Ephesians 4:23) and is able to be directly aware of God, demons, or angels.[5] Before the new birth, the spirit is real and has certain abilities to be aware of God. But most of the capacities of the unregenerate spirit are dead and inoperative. At the new birth, God implants or activates capacities in the spirit. These fresh capacities need to be nourished and developed so they can grow.

Think about a chest of drawers. Each drawer is a different compartment of the entire piece of furniture, and in each drawer is a group of resembling items—socks in one drawer, T-shirts in another; underwear, sweaters, and so on in their own drawers. In the same way, you are your soul (if you weren't, when you died and left your body, awaiting the future general resurrection, it wouldn't be you any longer!), but your soul has a number of "compartments" within it. You have a mind, a will, a body, and so forth.

Each of these compartments or faculties affect each other in very complicated ways. How you think can affect how you feel, and vice versa. What you believe affects what you choose, and vice versa. Your self-talk affects your mood. All of this means that there is a purely psychological aspect to all of one's faculties, as well as a distinctively spiritual aspect to each. Thus, based on a biblical understanding of the soul, we see that a holistic approach using therapy and spiritual development is crucial in alleviating the pain of anxiety.

It would be a profitable exercise to write down all of the faculties listed above and brainstorm how each one can affect the others. For example, in addressing anxiety, it may be important to train one's mind in a certain way, since the mind affects the faculty containing your feelings. Certain habitual patterns of self-talk trigger anxiety. If my mind constantly entertains fearful thoughts about the future, this will affect my emotional faculty by creating anxiety. But how about the soul-body connection? Do they affect each other?

THE BODY AND ITS RELATIONSHIP TO THE SOUL

The human body is an ensouled biological structure. This crucial point is best explained with an example. Suppose I had salt and a glass of water. If I put the salt in the water (and it dissolved), I would have salted water. If I could take the salt out of the water, there would be plain water left. In the example the salt = the soul, the salted water = the body, and plain water = a human corpse.

Note that the body is not merely a physical object. A body without a soul is, indeed, a mere physical object, and as such it is a mere corpse. It was a body, but no longer. The soul can exist without the body, just like salt can exist without salted water. But a body cannot exist without the soul, just like salted water cannot exist without salt. Remember, the body includes its physical, biological aspects—organs, cells, and so forth—but it also includes the soul fully present at every point where the body exists in order for it to be a body.

TWO CRUCIAL IMPLICATIONS FOR ADDRESSING ANXIETY/DEPRESSION

The implications of this cannot be overstated for developing a way—especially a Christian way—of addressing anxiety. Here I mention two: (1) The brain/nervous system can, in many cases, be helped by various anxiety-reducing medications prescribed by a psychiatrist or a primary care physician (e.g., antidepressants), and (2) the formation of habits that restructure the brain, the heart muscle, and other body parts can exchange the habit of being anxious with the habit of resting in peace and joy. These two implications are not exhaustive and are not meant to replace your professional care team's individualized strategy for you. But they were invaluable to me as I sought to better understand anxiety.

Regarding the first implication, while in the body, the soul needs the body to be functioning properly—the eyes, the brain, the nervous system—for it to work. The soul cannot see without the eyes working (at least while one is embodied). The emotions, including peace and joy instead of damaging anxiety, and the mind cannot work without the brain and nervous system working properly. Thus, anxiety is closely related to what is happening in the brain and nervous system. This means that antidepressants and other medications prescribed by a primary care physician or psychiatrist can, in many cases and under the proper guidance, return the brain to a more normal chemical balance so that anxiety is lessened or taken away altogether. It is important to realize that no one should feel the least bit embarrassed, unspiritual, or of little faith if one needs to take medications. Indeed, the idea of availing oneself of such help follows quite naturally from a holistic biblical anthropology.

Regarding the second implication, habit formation, we all know what it means to learn some particular activity—for example, to play golf or the piano. Consider golf. We start by becoming motivated to learn and by reading about how to play or by watching, say, a golf video. Yet no one in his or her right mind would stop at daily reading and videos! Practice is required.

Yet this is exactly our standard evangelical view of growing spiritually and psychologically and, by extension, of defeating anxiety. We think that if we hear the Bible preached once a week (twice if we're really committed!); if we read a bit of the Bible each day, as well as books on spiritual and psychological health; and if we listen to inspiring Christian music (the really committed even *sing* this music once in a while!), we'll really grow and anxiety will leave us. These activities are helpful and needed, but sufferers know they are not enough if one is dealing with anxiety.

Think of it like this. The intensity of anxiety or depression varies on a scale from light to severe. At some point on the scale, the intensity level is too high, and one may benefit significantly by including medications in one's approach.

Returning to the golf analogy, what is missing in this strategy? Practice, practice, practice. The really great players are those who keep practicing over the entire course of their careers. To learn golf, we go to a golf instructor at a driving range, and, focusing on specific movements under the instructor's direction, we repeat those movements over and over until a habit is formed. The same thing is done in learning how to play the piano, speak French, make pottery, or learn math. Sometimes we repeat a practice exercise that is not good in itself but is merely a means to getting good at the craft. One practices piano scales, not to get good at the scales, but to get good at playing complex musical scores.

So far, so good. But what does this have to do with flourishing as a follower of the Lord Jesus and replacing anxiety with peace and joy? A failure to answer that question—indeed, a failure even to ask it—has resulted in disaster for the church and countless disappointed, powerless, anxious, and depression-filled Christians. So we need to ask, What, specifically, does learning to play golf or the piano have to say to us about cultivating an anxiety-free life? Let's turn to Scripture to formulate an answer to this crucial question.

A number of New Testament texts seem a bit odd at first glance. It's hard to know how to take them if we do the right thing and interpret them literally. (Note: emphasis added in these texts below.)

> Therefore, I urge you, brothers and sisters, in view of God's mercy, to offer your *bodies* as a living sacrifice, holy and pleasing to God—this is your true and proper worship.
>
> *Romans 12:1*

This verse is unpacked earlier in Paul's letter:

> Even so, consider yourselves to be dead to sin, but alive to God in Christ Jesus. Therefore do not let sin reign in your mortal body so that you obey its lusts, and do not go on presenting the *members of your body* to sin as instruments of unrighteousness; but present yourselves to God as those alive from the dead, and *your members* as instruments of righteousness to God . . .

I am speaking in human terms because of the *weakness of your flesh*. For just as you *presented your members* as slaves to impurity and to lawlessness, resulting in further lawlessness, so now *present your members* as slaves to righteousness, resulting in sanctification.

Romans 6:11–13, 19 NASB

Do you not know that in a race all the runners run, but only one gets the prize? Run in such a way as to get the prize. Everyone who competes in the games *goes into strict training*. They do it to get a crown that will not last, but we do it to get a crown that will last forever. Therefore I do not run like someone running aimlessly. I do not fight like a boxer beating the air. No, I *strike a blow to my body and make it my slave* so that after I have preached to others, I myself will not be disqualified for the prize.

1 Corinthians 9:24–27

Therefore *consider the members of your earthly body* as dead to immorality, impurity, passion, evil desire, and greed, which amounts to idolatry.

Colossians 3:5 NASB

Train yourself to be godly. For *physical training* is of some value, but godliness has value for all things, holding promise for both the present life and the life to come.

1 Timothy 4:7–8

As mentioned above, at first glance, these texts—especially the italicized words—may seem a bit puzzling, but as we will now discover, they express insights about human nature, anxiety, and flourishing that are so deep that, once again, the insights of the Bible expose the shallowness of our own culture in breathtaking fashion. Properly understood, we will see that presenting two members of your body—your brain and your heart muscle—to God as instruments of righteousness (which includes emotional flourishing and overall health) can be important in replacing anxiety and worry with deep peace and joy. Learning how to present my brain and heart muscle in this way was a major source of transformation for me. Research has supported the idea that this can work.[6]

To understand this biblical teaching, we must first clarify four concepts: habit, character, flesh, and body.

A *habit* is an ingrained tendency to act, think, or feel a certain way without needing to choose to do so. The way a person writes the letters of the alphabet is not something he or she needs to think about. It is a habit, and one concentrates on what one is writing, not on the habitual style of handwriting used. *Character* is the sum total of one's habits, good and bad. Penmanship character is the sum total of one's good and bad writing habits; it is one's handwriting character.

Biblical terms such as *flesh* (*sarx*) and *body* (*soma*) have a wide field of meaning. Depending on the context, they can mean many different things. Sometimes *flesh* and *body* mean the same thing, but in the passages above, there is a unique and important meaning for each. *Body* is pretty obvious. In contrast to the soul, it refers to one's living, animated physical aspect. The body can be seen and touched, and it is composed of tissue, skin, and bone, as well as various organs (e.g., the heart) and systems (e.g., the nervous system). The *flesh* in these texts refers to the sinful tendencies or habits that reside in the body and whose nature is opposite that of the kingdom of God.[7] Flesh also seems to consist of powers that can dominate the soul and one's free will. In this case, flesh reigns over the soul.

To understand these more fully and to appreciate their importance more deeply, let's return to the example of learning to play golf. What I am about to say may sound a bit forced, but I mean for it to be taken quite literally.

When a person plays golf, he or she has a "golf character," that is, the sum of good and bad habits relevant for playing golf. One's "golf flesh" is the sum of one's bad golf habits. Where do these bad habits reside? They dwell as ingrained tendencies in specific body parts, particular members of the body that can be triggered unconsciously without one choosing to activate the habit(s). One's golf game may be weakened by bad habits in the wrists, the shoulders, or somewhere else. One may have good habits in one's legs, but bad habits—golf flesh—residing in one's shoulders. Golf flesh resides in the specific members of one's body.

How does one develop a good golf character? Not simply by daily golf readings coupled with regular exposure to motivational golf music. No, one must present one's members to a golf instructor at a driving range as instruments of golf "righteousness" instead of following one's golf flesh as an instrument of golf "unrighteousness." These are not figures of speech. They are literal indeed. By so presenting one's members, one gradually gets rid of bad golf habits and replaces them with good ones.

How does one present one's members to a golf instructor? Two things are involved. First, one must dedicate oneself to the pursuit of golf righteousness (to getting good at golf) and choose to submit as an apprentice to a master-teacher. Second, one does not simply engage in a one-time act of dedication to the master-teacher. To "present one's body" to a golf instructor requires repeatedly engaging specific body parts in regular activities done over and over again, with the instructor in charge, and practicing different movements.

For example, one may present the members of one's body, say, the wrists, to the instructor by practicing over and over again a specific wrist movement, a particular swing. The result of such habitual bodily movement will be the replacement of bad habits that dwell in the wrist with good habits. The golf flesh that resides in the wrists will give way to golf righteousness in those members. Later, the instructor may require the habitual presentation of other members, say, the hips, to replace bad habits that reside there.

A golf discipline is a repeated golf exercise, a bodily movement involving specific body parts, repeated over and over again, which is done for the purpose of getting rid of golf flesh and gaining golf righteousness in one's body. The important thing is this: a golf discipline is done repeatedly not to get good at the discipline, but to get good at the game of golf.

The parallels with becoming good at life (e.g., having a steady life of peace, joy, and little or no anxiety) should be clear. When one offers one's body to God as a living sacrifice (Romans 12:1), it involves not only a one-time act of dedication, but a habitual, repeated bodily exercise (1 Corinthians 9:24–27; 1 Timothy 4:7–8) involving specific body parts (Romans 6:12–13, 19), resulting in putting to death one's bad habits (Colossians 3:5), i.e., removing the flesh that resides in those body parts and replacing them with a righteousness that comes to reside in the members of one's body. A Christian spiritual discipline is a repeated bodily practice, done over and over again in dependence on the Holy Spirit and under the direction of Jesus and other wise teachers in his Way, to enable one to get good at certain things in life that one cannot do by direct effort.

In the same way that "golf flesh" resides in specific body parts, for example, the wrists, so sinful habits often reside in specific body parts, for example, anxiety primarily in the brain and nervous system, gossip in the tongue and mouth, and lust in the eyes. A spiritual discipline is a repetitive practice that targets one of these areas in order to replace bad habits with good ones in dependence on the Spirit of the living God.

Here is a specific application to anxiety, and one of the most crucial lessons I discovered: In some ways, anxiety is a learned habit that, through repeated flesh-forming activities (e.g., engaging in "what if?" thinking about the future and exaggerating what might happen if the "what if?" actually happens), forms grooves in the brain, heart muscle, and nervous system that trigger uncontrollable anxiety.

In neuroscience, the saying is, "Neurons that fire together wire together." In other words, repeated anxious thoughts, feelings, and actions cause certain neurons to fire together, and this repetition causes certain neurons to wire together to form ingrained circuits. Like muscle memory, these circuits are habit-triggering grooves. These anxiety-inducing grooves can be significantly eliminated and replaced by grooves that change the brain's circuitry, which, in turn, automatically trigger emotions of peace and joy. This replacement requires, among other things (e.g., a sense of community), repeated practice of certain activities that will be explained later.

HOW CONSCIOUS STATES LIKE ANXIETY ARE AND ARE NOT IN THE BODY

Before summarizing this chapter, I want to explain how conscious states—e.g., thoughts, memories, sensations—are and are not in the body. To begin with, it is important to say that here the methods and findings of neuroscience are unable to address the question and, in general, are largely irrelevant to important questions like, Is there a soul? Is consciousness physical or immaterial? What is anxiety itself?[8]

To see this, consider the discovery that if one's mirror neurons are damaged, then one cannot feel empathy for another. How are we to explain this? Three solutions come to mind. Each is fully consistent with all the scientific data, so those data cannot be used to decide which solution is more reasonable: (1) A feeling of empathy is the very same thing as the firings of mirror neurons; (2) a feeling of empathy is a genuinely immaterial state of consciousness in the brain that is caused by the firing of mirror neurons; or (3) a feeling of empathy is a genuinely immaterial state of consciousness in the soul—not the brain—that is caused by the firing of mirror neurons in the brain. No empirical scientific datum can pick out which of these three is correct. That issue is a philosophical and theological one, not a scientific matter.

Now consider a music CD (it would be more technically accurate to employ one of the old black vinyl records, but for communication purposes, I'll go with a CD). Strictly speaking, there is no music in the CD; there are only grooves. But if the CD is not damaged, when placed in the right retrieval system, the grooves trigger musical sounds. Remember, the body is an ensouled physical structure. The soul is fully present at each point of the body. Thus, for a human body to be a body, it must have a soulish and a physical dimension to it.

Now certain grooves associated with memories, thoughts, anxiety, and so forth are formed and stored in the physical dimension of the body. The physical aspect of the body is brute matter, and it cannot literally store conscious states. Brute matter is just the wrong type of thing to possess consciousness. But when these grooves are triggered, whether spontaneously by getting hit in the knee or by the mind searching to bring back a memory, the conscious state will obtain in the soulish aspect of the body. Since the soulish aspect of the body is just the soul being fully present at each point in the body, it is the soul that has conscious properties, not the physical body.

In the following chapters, I will refer back to points discussed in this chapter. I have found them to be crucial.

BULLET-POINT SUMMARY

- Extrabiblical knowledge is helpful for defeating anxiety and depression.
- The Bible's holistic, functional view of humanity implies that we should launch our attack against anxiety and depression by using tools that address all aspects of ourselves (e.g., medication to address the brain, psychology to address the mind or emotions, and biblical, spiritual practices to address the spirit).
- One of your faculties (e.g., the faculty of emotion) can impact positively or negatively other faculties (e.g., the faculty of desire, choice, mind).
- Anxiety and depression are related to what is happening in the brain, and medications may be of real help in treating them.
- Anxiety and depression are significantly formed habits residing in the brain and body, and they can be largely replaced with peaceful and joyful habits by regularly engaging in the right repetitive habit-forming exercises.

Chapter 2

GETTING A HANDLE ON ANXIETY/DEPRESSION

As I walked into the Dallas Seminary chapel one spring morning in 1976, my mind and body were riddled with fear, embarrassment, and deep loneliness. As I looked around at the thousand or so fellow students present that day, they all seemed so happy, so normal. And so many of them were married, some with little children. What was wrong with me? I was twenty-eight, and I was finishing my second of four years of seminary training. Why wasn't I married? Why wasn't I normal, like all the other students?

I was also finishing my second year of dating a beautiful, godly young woman of my age who was on the Campus Crusade staff in Dallas. The problem was I had an "approach and avoidance" disorder. The closer I got to asking her to marry me, the more afraid and anxious I became. So I would back off a bit. With a little distance, I felt the urge to move closer to her and draw near to getting engaged again. This had gone on for two years.

She was certain we were going to get married, and I so wanted to be there. Little did I know that my struggle was related to my father dying when I was a child. As a result, I was subconsciously afraid to get too close to someone for fear of being hurt again. But this gal was quite a catch. Thank God, I eventually worked through my problem, got engaged the next January, and Hope and I were married on May 14, 1977 (yes, I remember!). But when I walked into the chapel that spring day in 1976, I was far from having worked things out. I felt very anxious that day. What was wrong with me? Why was everyone else happy and I wasn't? Why did I fight anxiety when my fellow students seemed untouched by this wicked enemy? And here I was, approaching thirty, and I couldn't settle on a wife, like so many of my colleagues had. I felt different, messed up, and alone.

THINGS TO KNOW ABOUT ANXIETY/DEPRESSION

But was I? If you or a loved one has struggled with significant anxiety, you or your loved one know what it is like to feel isolated, different (in a bad way), hopeless, and full of fear. As a result, we need to learn a few things about our enemy. First, you are not alone. In 2003, 15 percent of the US population between the ages of eighteen and fifty-four (forty million people) suffered from an anxiety disorder.[1] Since then, the numbers have increased. Anxiety disorders are the most common mental illness in America, and they affect women and teenagers especially hard (besides posttraumatic stress disorder, women are twice as likely as men to have an anxiety disorder). More generally, anxiety disorders affect around one out of every thirteen people.[2]

In 2017, Dr. Joseph Mercola had this to say:

Anxiety is the new depression, with more than half of all American college students reporting anxiety. Recent research shows anxiety—characterized by constant and overwhelming worry and fear—is now 800 percent more prevalent than all forms of cancer.

A 2016 report by the Center for Collegiate Mental Health at Penn State confirmed the trend, finding anxiety and depression are the most common concerns among college students who seek counseling. Data from the National Institute of Mental Health (NIMH) suggests the prevalence of anxiety disorders in the U.S. may be as high as 40 million, or about 18 percent of the population over the age of 18, making it the most common mental illness in the nation.[3]

I am among those who do not believe that "the percentage of people who have anxiety has always held pretty constant; rather, it's just that today we're more open to speaking about it." No, I am convinced that the anxiety (and depression) rate is higher today than it has ever been. Why? Because the conditions present today in American culture—e.g., the rapid pace at which we live, the bombardment we receive from all kinds of readily available technology, the isolation we experience in a hyperindividualistic society—are so extreme that we are living with stress, stress, and more stress. Indeed, we are so used to being under stress that we hardly recognize it much of the time. One of the greatest, if not *the* greatest, causes of serious anxiety is stress.

Despite all this, there is good news: statistics also show there is reasonable hope to significantly minimize or even get rid of disabling anxiety if you do the right things.

There is a very important coping device in these statistics. *I'm alone; I'm a sicko; I'm a hopeless cause; I'm a failure as a Christian*—the next time thoughts like these come into your awareness, remember that they are lies! Change your self-talk to reflect the truth: You are a normal member of society, along with millions like you, and you live in a very stressful culture that is so individualistic that community and friendships are rare. Yet if you do the right things, it is quite likely you will make solid progress.

Call this to mind if you are in need and feel alone or picked on by God:

> No trial or hardship has overtaken you except what is common to mankind.
>
> *1 Corinthians 10:13, my paraphrase*

> Resist [the devil], standing firm in the faith, because you know that the family of believers throughout the world is undergoing the same kind of sufferings.
>
> *1 Peter 5:9*

Rather than isolating us from one another, our suffering—especially suffering from anxiety or depression—can connect us with others. As psychologist Kristin Neff wisely observes, "When we're in touch with our common humanity, we remember that feelings of inadequacy and disappointment are shared by all. This is what distinguishes self-compassion from self-pity. Whereas self-pity says 'poor me,' self-compassion remembers that everyone suffers, and it offers comfort because everyone is human. The pain I feel in difficult times is the same pain that you feel in difficult times."[4]

Neff's comments remind us that we dare not let anxiety or depression isolate us from others. In point of fact, we need just the opposite. Group therapy, a support group at church, and deepening relationships with safe and caring friends and family are all important in getting well.

What is anxiety? It is a feeling of uneasiness, apprehension, or nervousness. It always has a trigger, but we often don't know what that trigger is or what we're anxious about (in the next chapter, I will offer practical steps to get better at this).[5] There are several different kinds of anxiety disorder, including generalized anxiety disorder, social anxiety, phobic, posttraumatic stress, and separation anxiety disorders.[6] I am not qualified to address the specific aspects of these disorders. But be encouraged. I have learned some things about generalized anxiety disorder (GAD), panic disorder, and obsessive-compulsive disorder that you may find helpful. And much of it can be useful for certain aspects of other anxiety disorders as well.

What causes anxiety? I offer this list so you can engage in an exercise. You may want to read slowly through the list with pen and paper in hand, note the factor or factors that seem most relevant to your situation (rank them in order of importance if you can), and jot down some initial thoughts about what you can do to engage properly those factors:[7]

- genetic predispositions
- parenting (overprotective, overcontrollers, inconsistent responders)

- early childhood experiences that fostered shame or insecurity
- current lifestyle (especially stress, stress, stress; but also unanticipated threats, escalating demands, confidence killers, terrorizing trauma, significant change)
- the inability to predict or control the future as much as you would like

Do one or more of these factors apply to you? Most likely, the answer is yes. Then you can try to get to the root of these factors.

In addition to defining anxiety, listing its different forms, and noting many of its causes, there is another aspect of anxiety I found important to know: anxiety is a surface feeling that masks the deeper feelings that are most likely the real issue you are dealing with—embarrassment, fear, grief, helplessness, hurt, loneliness, or sadness.[8] Feelings are like bubbles—we need to let them rise to the surface (not stuff them or fight them) and be open to what surfaces. Then we can experience and release them as they move through us like letting air out of a balloon. Feelings may also be likened to waves. We needn't be afraid the wave will swell and overwhelm us, but can instead let it pass by and ride it out. The feeling touches us and will eventually leave. It is especially helpful to remember this while experiencing a panic attack.

It is my heartfelt passion that God will use this book to point people who are suffering anxiety to sources of relief. But that won't happen if you read through the book without reflecting on your own experiences. So again, I urge you to look at the list of deeper feelings and seek to discover which apply to you and why.

Finally, don't waste your suffering. Anxiety or depression can be occasions for formation or deformation, for becoming stronger in the long run or weaker. So do what you can—even if it's a baby step—to resolve to let all of this work together for your good. And the good news is that studies have demonstrated beyond a reasonable doubt that you can substantially lessen or get rid of your anxiety and increase your happiness.

My favorite radio talk show host is Dennis Prager. He regularly reminds his listeners that they have a moral duty to be happy. Why? Because happy people lift the spirits of those around them; they make the lives of others better; they are more productive in life; and they are psychologically and physically healthier than those who are not happy. I mention this not to shame or pour guilt on anyone who struggles with being happy. Such manipulation is deeply wrong, and besides, feeling shame or guilt seldom does anyone any good. Rather, I mention the moral duty to be happy to encourage you to take seriously the step of setting a goal to improve in your happiness.

In her masterful work *The How of Happiness*, psychology professor Sonja Lyubomirsky asks the question, "What determines happiness?"[9] Here are what research studies have found: Fifty percent of what determines people's happiness is accounted for by their inherited, biological set points. Some people are born happier than others. Only about 10 percent of what determines happiness is due to life circumstances. You may think this is far too low, but if you reflect for a moment, it becomes evident that circumstances are subject to the law of diminishing returns. If you get married, get a raise at work, and experience a host of other good things happening to you, it will usually only take a few months or so for the newness to wear off. This law of diminishing returns is the basic cause of addiction, e.g., to pornography, alcohol, or drugs.

At first, a little bit will give a person the adrenaline rush they seek. But after a while, the law of diminishing returns sets in, and they need more of the addicting item to get the same pleasure. And on it goes. Now this doesn't mean everyone should intentionally seek miserable circumstances! But we have to change our thinking about the importance of circumstances. It has been shown that they only contribute to a measly 10 percent of people's happiness quotient. Knowing this eases the pressure to change one's circumstances, come what may, as a cure for anxiety and unhappiness.

Finally, 40 percent of one's happiness quotient is due to—are you ready for this—*intentional free choices.* I actually wonder if the 50 percent number for an inherited happiness set point is too high, and if the percentage of one's happiness due to exercising free will to make good choices ought to be higher. But even at 40 percent, do you see what this means? You have it in your power to begin a regimen of choices, assuming that you choose the right things and form a habit of this, that can substantially improve your happiness and decrease or get rid of your anxiety. There really is hope. And in the remaining chapters, I will get specific about what I did to make progress, not because the sources of help that I found will work for everyone, but as ideas to consider and encouragement that there are steps everyone can take to improve their happiness.

READ WITH SELF-COMPASSION

Before we launch into specifics in the next chapter, I have a very important idea I want to get before your mind and heart. As you read what follows, do so with a heart of compassion—tenderness, kindness, acceptance—for yourself, with a desire for health and flourishing (well-being) for yourself. Why do I suggest this? Because I agree with psychologist Kristin Neff when she writes, "Insecurity, anxiety, and depression are incredibly common in our society, and much of this is due to self-judgment, to beating ourselves up when we feel we aren't winning in the game of life."[10]

It's actually all right with God if you are nice to yourself! Rather than experiencing your anxiety or depression as an occasion for self-loathing and condemning yourself for being such a failure, you can experience it as an opportunity to soften your heart toward yourself. Seek to have an open heart toward yourself with gentleness. After all, we are all flawed and fragile! Your anxiety or depression is simply a part of common humanity—we all have these same or closely related problems.

You may be among those Christians who cringe at this idea. You may think that such an attitude is really a self-centered, unbiblical narcissism that is consistent with the thought that life is all and only about the self-lover.[11] Or you may fear that if you adopt an attitude of self-compassion, you will be too easy on yourself, let yourself off the hook too easily and prematurely, stop growing in Christ, and fail to deal with sin in your life.

It's true that Jesus was very clear on the second greatest commandment in the Bible: "Love your neighbor as yourself" (Mark 12:31). This seems to imply that we are to start by loving ourselves and then love others in that same way, very much like Jesus' instructions to "do to others as you would have them do to you" (Luke 6:31). Surely Jesus would not want us to reject self-love for self-loathing and love others in a harsh way!

Yet Jesus clearly affirms the centrality of self-love and compassion in two other texts. In the Mark passage cited above, Jesus is quoting from Leviticus 19:18. In the context of Leviticus 19:13–17, we are warned not to oppress ("to keep someone in hardship; to cause distress, anxiety, or discomfort to") our neighbor, judge our neighbor unjustly, slander our neighbor, hate our neighbor in our hearts, and take revenge or bear a grudge against our neighbor. Rather, we are to love our neighbor as we love ourselves, implying that self-love is first and is inconsistent with these attitudes and actions toward others. Again, in Romans 13:9, Paul repeats Leviticus 19:18 and simply adds in verse 10 that love "does no harm to a neighbor," presumably because one would not do a wrong to oneself.

If I'm right about this, then we already have the beginnings of a definition of self-compassion. It involves (1) adopting feelings and attitudes toward oneself that are not oppressive and harsh, (2) setting aside being inordinately self-judgmental by giving oneself messages that are self-condemning—e.g., I am such a failure—and produce shame and guilt, (3) not slandering and demeaning oneself, and (4) not beating oneself up and holding a grudge against oneself. In short, not wronging ourselves in any way. Rather, we are to direct the very opposite of these feelings and behaviors toward ourselves.

Psychologist Marina Krakovsky defines the most basic level of self-compassion to mean "treating yourself with the same kindness and understanding that you would a friend."[12] She goes on to say that people who struggle with self-compassion "do not necessarily lack compassion toward others. Rather they hold themselves to higher standards than they would expect of anyone else."

According to Krakovsky, the following is an initial way to determine whether or not you have self-compassion:

Statements associated with high self-compassion:

- I try to see my failings as part of the human condition.
- When I'm going through a very hard time, I try to keep my emotions in balance.
- I try to be understanding and patient toward those aspects of my personality that I don't like.

Statements linked to low self-esteem:

- When I fail at something important to me, I become consumed by feelings of inadequacy.
- When I'm feeling down, I tend to feel like most other people are probably happier than I am.
- I'm disapproving and judgmental about my own flaws and inadequacies.[13]

It may be worthwhile to take a minute and rank each of the six statements on a scale of 1 ("I never say this") to 10 ("this describes my self-talk perfectly"). Then, while being gentle and accepting of yourself, assess your strengths and weaknesses. After you've done this, practice the following exercise in self-talk: Start describing yourself with the statements associated with high self-esteem, even if you don't believe them. This is not hypocritical as long as you truly desire to believe them and see the practice of these self-descriptions as a way to fulfill that desire. Regarding the statements of low self-esteem, as various ideas are presented in the following pages, you may want to return and examine these statements.

Interestingly, according to psychologists, there are three indispensable aspects to self-compassion, and all of them are deeply biblical: (1) kindness toward yourself in difficult times (see Mark 12:31; 1 Corinthians 13:4); (2) paying attention to your suffering in a mindful, nonobsessive way (and Psalm 139:23–24 would add that we invite God to examine us as a colaborer in this self-mindfulness); and (3) common humanity, or the recognition that your suffering is a part of the human experience rather than unique to you (see 1 Peter 5:9).

It is crucial to recognize that self-compassion is different from self-esteem. As Kristin Neff warns, the emphasis on self-esteem in our culture leads to all kinds of "traps that people can fall into when they try to get and keep a sense of high self-esteem: narcissism, self-absorption, self-righteous anger, prejudice, discrimination, and so on. I realized that self-compassion was the perfect alternative to the relentless pursuit of self-esteem. Why? Because it offers the same protection against harsh self-criticism as self-esteem, but without the need to see ourselves as perfect or as better than others. *In other words, self-compassion provides the same benefits as high self-esteem without its drawbacks.*"[14]

Before we finish this chapter, let's return to the two main problems people have with self-compassion: it's narcissistic, and it causes people to be indulgent with themselves so they don't grow. Regarding narcissism, the first response to this problem is that, as we have seen, the Bible teaches the importance of self-love and even uses it as a standard for how to treat others. But the Bible would never affirm narcissism, so the two cannot be the same thing.

Second, narcissism means excessive self-interest, egotism, self-centeredness, and self-absorption, along with a craving for admiration. But biblical self-love is contrary to all these. For one thing, biblical self-love is nothing like self-centeredness and the like. Rather, it sets self-love in the context of love for God and neighbor. For another, narcissists are dismissive of others because "it's all about me!" This is the opposite of biblical self-love.

Third, narcissism expresses a grandiose personality type that is reflective of a mental disorder. But biblical self-love is the healthy, right thing to do. I recognize that I have high value as one who is made in the image of God; that in Christ, there is absolutely no more condemnation toward me (Romans 8:1); and that I am so treasured by God that he has lavished his love on me (1 John 3:1). I could go on, but I think the point has been made: biblical self-love is the only sensible response to what God has made us to be and to how he feels about us.

What about the idea that self-love causes us to let ourselves off the hook too easily and leads to self-indulgence? Scientific studies have actually shown just the opposite. People with healthy self-love are far more motivated to grow, to do well in various activities, and have a greater zest for life than those without self-compassion.[15] Furthermore, people with self-compassion are more resilient and better able to regain emotional well-being after adversity and are less prone to anxiety and depression.

In closing, here are some practical ideas for increasing your self-compassion. Each time you pick up this book to read, take a moment to remind yourself that the time has come to stop being too hard on yourself and beating yourself up. Tell yourself, "I'm too precious to be stuck in anxiety and depression. I am worthy of a life of peace, joy, and security in the Lord. And with his help, I will have this!"

When you "fail," do something stupid, or give yourself a reason for self-condemnation, stop for a moment and think of someone about whom you care deeply—a close friend or a family member. Now ask what your attitude would be toward them if you found out they did the very thing for which you are condemning yourself. Most likely, you would reach out to the person and seek to comfort them and offer them positive emotions and supportive talk. Now, take that very same attitude and set of actions and apply them to yourself.

Practice forming a relaxed, gentle attitude toward yourself.

There are two ways to do this. First, practice the presence of a gentle God, because *he is that way.* Second, in order to learn to be gentle to something, such as a puppy, you need to see it as simultaneously precious and vulnerable.[16] Practice ways to see yourself as both, especially using these terms and the attitudes they express in your self-talk. If one of the two ideas (or both) are an obstacle for you and you just can't think of yourself this way, try to find and pray about what is blocking you.

Self-compassion requires that you clearly bring to mind and openly admit to yourself the suffering you have endured at various times. When we see someone suffering, this tends to draw out our compassion for that person. The same is true when it comes to having compassion for our own suffering.

Bullet-Point Summary

- If you have anxiety, you are not alone, weird, a spiritual failure, or hopeless.
- Stress, stress, stress is a major cause of anxiety. Get rid of it!
- There is reasonable hope that you can defeat anxiety.
- Among the several causes of anxiety, select the ones with which you most identify.
- Anxiety is a surface feeling that often hides deeper feelings—embarrassment, fear, grief, helplessness, hurt, loneliness, sadness. With which do you most identify?
- Don't waste your suffering.
- You have a moral duty to be happy.

- By adopting a certain approach to life, one that includes the proper regimen of habit-forming practices, you can defeat anxiety and become much happier.
- Self-compassion is an appropriate, biblically based feeling and attitude to take toward yourself. There are certain exercises that enhance self-compassion.
- Cultivate the habit of making intentional free choices that produce peace and well-being.

Chapter 3

SPIRITUAL AND PSYCHOLOGICAL TOOLS FOR DEFEATING ANXIETY/ DEPRESSION:

PART 1

Neuroplasticity, Habit Formation, and Anxiety/Depression

As I write this (June 10, 2017), a *New York Times* article was just posted online. The title of the article is "Prozac Nation Is Now the United States of Xanax."[1] The article begins by quoting Sarah Fader, a thirty-seven-year-old social media consultant living in Brooklyn, New York. Fader herself has GAD (generalized anxiety disorder), the same disorder I inherited. According to Fader, "If you are a human being living in 2017 and you're not anxious, there's something wrong with you." The article goes on to note that as depression was to the 1990s, we have now entered a new age of anxiety. Fader's remark was surely tongue-in-cheek, and depression is, sadly, still among us. But one thing seems certain: the very conditions of life in America make anxiety an inevitable epidemic. That's the bad news.

The good news is that, as I have repeatedly said, change is possible if we go about it in the correct way. One of the most important things about each of us is our *habits*—thoughts, feelings, and behaviors—that we do (or have) without choosing to do (or have) them and, often, without even knowing a habit has been triggered. Anxiety is largely a habit wired or grooved into one's brain and nervous system that becomes activated when one encounters certain triggers. To minimize or get rid of anxiety, I've learned it is absolutely crucial that one recognizes bad, anxiety-producing habits and undertakes a training program that, over time, rids one of those bad habits and replaces them with good ones. If this is done correctly and for several months (e.g., two to six months), one's brain and nervous system can literally change their structure and develop new grooves that constitute new anxiety-defeating habits.

Neuroplasticity refers to the brain's ability to form new brain grooves (i.e., new patterns of synaptic connections) and undergo a change of structure. The brain is not stuck in a static, unchanging structure. In fact, through repeated habit-forming practices of different ways of thinking, feeling, and behaving, one can reshape one's brain in a healthy direction. But this reshaping requires three things: practice, practice, practice! Practice doesn't make perfect; it makes permanent. Through repeated practice, a new set of grooves becomes relatively permanent, unless one retreats into old, bad habits. And this is especially true of anxiety. Through proper practice, one can literally train one's brain automatically to trigger good thoughts, feelings, and behavioral habits that happen without one having to choose them intentionally. For example, through certain practices, you can change from being a half-empty to a half-full (or completely full!) person.

While thinking, feeling, and behaving habits are all important, I want to focus in this chapter on practical ways of retraining one's anxiety-producing thinking habits. Why? As Dallas Willard reminded us, "Feelings have a crucial role in life, but they must not be taken as a basis for action or character change. That role falls to insight, understanding, and conviction of truth."[2] The centrality of one's thought life for the condition of one's emotional well-being is a consistent theme of the Bible. Take a few minutes to meditate on these passages:

> For as he thinks within himself, so he is.
>
> *Proverbs 23:7 NASB*

> Do not conform to the pattern of this world, but be transformed by the renewing of your mind.
>
> *Romans 12:2*

> We take captive every thought to make it obedient to Christ.
>
> *2 Corinthians 10:5*

> Finally, brothers and sisters, whatever is true, whatever is noble, whatever is right, whatever is pure, whatever is lovely, whatever is admirable—if anything is excellent or praiseworthy—think about such things.
>
> *Philippians 4:8*

> Set your minds on things above, not on earthly things.
>
> *Colossians 3:2*

Without question, these and many other texts establish the importance to our overall well-being of how we train our minds and of what our minds habitually dwell on. As psychologists Edmund Bourne and Lorna Garano remind us: "The truth is that *it's what we say to ourselves* [the self-talk of our thought life] *in response to any particular situation that mainly determines our mood and feelings.*"[3]

Now while these Bible verses are clear and even wonderful, for years I found them very frustrating because no one told me how to follow them! If this has been your frustration as well, then what follows may be of real help to you, as it has been to me. This chapter's focus is to provide simple spiritual and psychological habit-forming practices that can empower and enlighten you on how increasingly to internalize these verses. The ideas to follow have been central to my own recovery from clinical anxiety. If I had to pick a chapter in this book that is the most important, it would be this one.

GETTING RID OF ANXIETY/ DEPRESSION-PRODUCING AND HABITUAL NEGATIVE THINKING

A I mentioned in the last chapter, a major source—if not *the* major source—of negative emotions like anxiety is what preoccupies our minds when they are in their default position. This is the place to which your mind automatically reverts when you aren't intensely focused on a specific topic or activity. The default position is made up of the thoughts that fill our minds, usually almost subconsciously, as a result of habitually going there to cope with hurt, embarrassment, fear, and so forth. And the major aspect of the default position is the enslaving, debilitating, negative self-talk one constantly expresses: *I am such a loser. Why did I say that at the meeting yesterday? What if such and such happens next week? I'll be in real trouble. I never do things right. I'm vulnerable. I'm not good enough. The world is dangerous.* And on and on. Remember, many of these are so subtle and almost silent, and we are so used to talking to ourselves this way and believing what they say that they pass through or settle in our minds without us noticing they are there. Yet if left alone, they lead to anxiety, depression, and social withdrawal. How in the world can we stop this negative self-talk?

The Four-Step Solution
Introducing the Four-Step Solution

Christian neuroscientist and UCLA professor Jeffrey Schwartz and psychiatrist Rebecca Gladding have provided a four-step practice that in my experience actually works.[4] I have been practicing daily the Four-Step Solution for more than two years, and it has ushered into my soul daily peace and joy while banishing almost all of my significant and inappropriate anxiety. And while Schwartz and Gladding's book is written to a general audience, reference is regularly made to Christian teaching and the Holy Spirit, and the four steps are biblically rooted. I will list the four steps, elaborate on them, and make their habitual application easy to do.

Examining the Four-Step Solution

1. STEP 1: RELABELING. Your thoughts are simply uncomfortable, deceptive, destructive brain messages that are mere habits of yours with no connection to reality. Call these messages what they really are.

2. STEP 2: REFRAMING. Take the power out of the thoughts as you change your perception of the importance of the deceptive brain message by (1) being mindful, in cooperation with the Holy Spirit, by actively focusing your attention on the deceptive brain message to become fully aware that you are having it, what its content is, and how you are currently feeling; and (2) labeling the message correctly under one of the major types of distorted thinking patterns (see below).

3. STEP 3: REFOCUSING. Refocus your attention on something that distracts you and gets you into a flow—move on. Flow occurs when you are so focused on something that you lose track of time and what's going on around you. The key is not to ruminate about the message, arguing with yourself why it isn't true or drawing out horrible implications of it. Such rumination, even telling yourself why the message isn't true, actually deepens the brain grooves that trigger the message and makes it harder to get rid of. The goal is to dismiss the message that is disempowered by steps 1 and 2.

4. STEP 4: REVALUING. After a while and when it is safe to go back and reflect on your employment of steps 1–3, think about what you did, be strengthened by what you did well, learn from your mistakes, and recommit yourself to doing this repeatedly throughout each day to make all of this a habit.

STEP 1: *Relabeling*

Let's reflect a bit on these steps, starting with step 1. Your brain sends you false messages all throughout the day, and many of them are destructive and anxiety-producing. The trick is to learn to become aware of them instead of letting them be present but under the radar and to start disempowering the message by labeling it a false brain habit triggered by a groove in your brain with no connection to reality. It is habituated distorted thinking that, through repetition of negative self-talk, has now dug a deep groove in your brain, a rut that is triggered largely through habit. It is important, then, to exert the effort to go through your day and become more aware of the presence of these messages than you have been. I don't know about you, but I have needed help with that, especially so I don't let step 1 become overfocused, harmful introspection in which I am constantly taking my own anxiety temperature!

So, what do we do to practice step 1 most helpfully? My therapist friend Bill Roth always says that we should not go scuba diving alone (i.e., go inward via introspection). Always invite God to go with you and to bring to your awareness any sensations you are having. Thus, Psalm 139:23–24 provides both a biblical basis for step 1 and offers us guidance for practicing it wisely: "Search me, God, and know my heart; test me and know my anxious thoughts. See if there is any offensive way in me, and lead me in the way everlasting." Wow, is this perfect or what! It fits steps 1 and 2 like a hand in a glove.

The notion of "the way everlasting" is clarified in Psalm 16:11, where the writer implies God's revelation of a (surely Christ-honoring) healthy path of life, associated especially with fullness of joy and the experience of delightful pleasures from God both now and into the future. These are not mere words. They can become a reality if you really intend to have them replace anxiety by staying on a course in which you form new habituated grooves that trigger these thoughts and feelings and replace negative self-talk and anxiety. Step 1 is the beginning of the journey toward taking the power away from a deceptive brain message.

Step 1 is especially important as the beginning step for dealing with a specific, debilitating, fearful, thought-filled emotion—e.g., being anxious (or depressed) about getting anxious (or depressed). Anyone with significant anxiety or depression will tell you that one of the hardest, yet most damaging, things to get rid of is the fear of getting anxious or depressed again. In fact, therapists note that one of the most common triggers of significant anxiety/depressive episodes is when one starts thinking about one's own anxiety or depression and then starts getting worried, fearful, or anxious about having another anxiety/depressive episode!

I have done this many, many times. But step 1 places you on the beginning of a pathway that, with practice, will turn you away from giving such second-order thoughts the time of day. In this way, they do not get the opportunity to build up anticipatory fear in your mind. Rather, they become passing thoughts that you simply dismiss and move on.

STEP 2: *Reframing*

Step 2 goes even deeper in stripping the power from such a message. I have heard it said that if a hospital patient can simply be given a name or label for what is causing him or her pain, it actually lessens the pain. And that is the idea that underlies step 2. While inviting the Holy Spirit in through praying Psalm 139:23–24, step 2 urges us to become so aware of the thought and its associated feeling that we can give a name or label to the thought. Among other things, this gives us a genuine sense of power over it. And it reminds us that we are not alone in suffering from this habit of thinking. Rather, it fits a category in which numerous other people engage. Here is a fairly standard list of distorted thinking traps:[5]

1. All-or-nothing thinking. (If you're not perfect or if you get anything wrong, you're a total failure.)
2. Overgeneralizing. ("I always do that.")
3. Mental filter. (You pick out a single negative detail and dwell on it.)
4. Discounting the positive. (If you did a good job, you tell yourself that anyone could have done it.)
5. Jumping to conclusions or mind reading. (You interpret others' actions, tone of voice, or body language in a negative way or, like fortune-telling, you assume and predict that others don't like you and that things will turn out badly.)
6. Magnification or catastrophizing. (You exaggerate your weaknesses or the harmful aspects of events that

have happened or may happen, thus minimizing your strengths or the odds that the event will never happen and, even if it did, the results won't be that bad.)

7. Emotional reasoning. (You actually believe that reality is the way you feel.)

8. Inappropriate "should" statements. ("I should avoid being around people because they will see what a loser I am.")

9. Self-labeling. ("I made a mistake, so I am a loser.")

10. Self-blame. (You blame yourself for events outside your control.)

I have done all of these, but, if I may say so humbly, I am a world-class expert at magnification or catastrophizing. The reason I am so good at it is that I combine it with "what if?" thinking. What if something happens to my grandchildren? I'm sure it will be horrible and beyond my ability to cope with it! Until the last two years or so, I have spent most of my life living in the future. But not anymore. On Sunday, I look at my calendar to be sure my week is planned appropriately, and then I take one day at a time. I'm being honest here. For the past two and a half years, my wife will ask me what I have going on this week or when my next ministry trip is, and I tell her, "Honey, I have absolutely no idea." And I mean it!

Now, you would think that when Jesus offers us guidance about life, it would be good for us, wouldn't you? Well, recall this warning: "Therefore do not worry about tomorrow, for tomorrow will worry about itself. Each day has enough trouble of its own" (Matthew 6:34). We all recognize the good in this and hunger to be this way. Think of the anxiety that would simply go away if we were like this. Haven't you wanted to know how to do this?

It certainly isn't by sheer willpower. As Dallas Willard wrote, "No one can succeed in mastering feelings in his or her life who tries to simply take them head-on and resist or redirect them by 'willpower' in the moment of choice."[6] But if you want to internalize Jesus' advice, I've found you can actually do so by practicing the Four-Step Solution over and over again for two to six months. If done with effort and consistency, this approach to life becomes second nature. By practicing the habit-forming Four-Step Solution, you can learn to live in the present and gain the ability to avoid "what if?" catastrophic thinking about the future. Besides, some experts estimate that 85 percent of the things we worry about never happen![7] And the negative things that do happen are usually not as bad as we anticipated.

STEP 3: *Refocusing*

Step 3 may be the most important one for tapping in to the neuroplasticity of the brain and changing its negative grooves to positive ones. Once steps 1 and 2 have disempowered the negative brain message, it is important to adopt a dismissive attitude toward it and then follow-up by actually dismissing the thought. You say to your distorted thought, "I know who you are. You are just a habit, a false habit that I can actually name. You are an example of emotional reasoning. You have nothing to do with reality, and I'm not going to waste my time entertaining you. I have better things to do right now. So, good-bye!"

At that point, you turn to some distracting activity to remove your focus on the brain message. It can be anything— taking a walk, reading something, listening to music, calling a friend, watching television, surfing the internet, checking emails—just as long as it engages you and brings about flow.

STEP 4: *Revaluing*

After a while, you can return to the dismissed and out-of-mind message and reevaluate (step 4) how steps 1–3 went. You will want to make sure that you can revisit the false brain message (step 1) without it retaining the power to agitate you again. If you find that it does, go back to what you were doing in step 3 or to some other activity that puts you in the flow again. The goal here is to be away from the false brain message long enough that you can go back to it in your mind without experiencing the negative emotions associated with it.

When you find that you're able to do this—and it will take trial and error, along with many mistakes, before you learn your own pacing—reevaluate steps 1–3. Think of what you did that was helpful or unhelpful. Based on this, ponder what you can do next time to improve your skills and benefit more fully from steps 1–3. As you do, remember that when learning to form any new habit, you are not likely to be very good at things until you have practiced for a few months. After months of practicing these steps (with a lot of failure), I have found that step 4 becomes less important.

Summary Thoughts about the Four-Step Solution

The important thing about step 3 is that it keeps us from ruminating about the false message. Ruminating just reinforces and deepens the brain groove that habitually triggers negative self-talk, and it makes it harder to stop. However, I should make an important point of clarification here. One of the most common therapeutic approaches to anxiety is cognitive behavioral therapy (CBT). It involves identifying the negative message, analyzing it (asking questions like, From the list presented earlier, what kind of cognitive distortion is this? What is it about this message that I find upsetting? Does this remind me of something in my past that bothered me?), and raising counterevidence against the message (asking questions like, What's the evidence for this? Is this always true? Has this really been true in the past?).

This raises the question: How do cognitive behavioral therapy and the Four-Step Solution relate to each other? I suggest the following that has been immensely helpful to me. If an anxiety-inducing message occurs and it's relatively new, then I've found the CBT approach is appropriate. A message can be kept from becoming habitual if I analyze it carefully and embrace reasons not to believe it. But if a false brain message is *habitual*—it is a regular visitor of yours—then I think the time has come to use the four-step approach.

One more point. Step 1 says that the brain message is false and has no connection to reality. But you may think to yourself that, indeed, you find the message to have a lot of truth to it. It has often been true in the past ("people always abandon me"), and step 1 is trying to make me pretend the message is just false. Here's my response. First, how has it been working for you to take these regular self-talk visitors as the sober truth? Probably not so well. So, what would it hurt to try a different approach for a while? Second, given that you are now anxious from the message, it is likely that your ascription of truth to it is an example of distorted thinking patterns 2, 3, 6, and 7 above (see pages 74–75) and maybe others. In this case, you are not in a good position to assess accurately the degree of truth to the brain message, so it is wiser to trust the method and go with it rather than with your own intuitions.

THE HEARTMATH SOLUTION
The Importance of the Heart Organ in the Bible and Science

I thank God for the Four-Step Solution. It has helped many people, including me, find freedom from anxiety. But the problem that needs discussing in this precise context is that some people's anxiety is due to an obsessive-compulsive disorder in which one has obsessive thoughts that they cannot let go of. And even if we don't have this disorder, it is still true that some thoughts are so terrifying to us that we obsess on them and cannot move on. In these difficult cases, the Four-Step Solution seems impotent. What should one do in these cases to avoid anxiety?[8]

Fortunately, there is a habit-forming practice first discovered by medical doctors that is tailor-made for just this sort of situation. In the medical literature, it is called the HeartMath Solution.[9] So as a natural follow-up to the previous section,

I want to introduce you to the HeartMath Solution, a kind of meditation that may well be new to you. It is regularly used by medical doctors, psychiatrists, and therapists. I have found it to be life-giving.

This sort of meditation weaves together three strands, two biblical and one scientific. Besides meditating on specific biblical texts, there are two scriptural strands of meditation sometimes overlooked. In the first scriptural strand, we are also urged to meditate on general abstract themes in Scripture, for example, on agape love, on justice, on hope, and so forth. Thus, the apostle Paul wisely urges that "whatever is true, whatever is noble, whatever is right, whatever is pure, whatever is lovely, whatever is admirable—if anything is excellent or praiseworthy—think about such things" (Philippians 4:8). Certainly, we would want to remember and meditate on God's wonderful acts toward us and those we care about. Remembering the times we received or gave of ourselves in love or extended forgiveness, times when the presence of God was especially precious, and answers to prayer—these are also proper objects for meditation.

Along these same lines, we could meditate on anything that is edifying and encourages us toward a life of Christian maturity and gratitude toward God, whether grand or small. And God's creation is a vast repository of objects to ponder and to offer thanks to God about, such as attending to the sound of rain, to ducks swimming in a pond, or even to the wonderful tastes of what we eat. When one is anxious and depressed, the so-called grand things of life may be difficult to hold one's attention. But anyone can start by being thankful for the taste of one's morning coffee or a glass of orange juice. How wonderful of God to create a world with such gratuitous pleasures!

A second important scriptural strand involves the nature and role of the heart in a life of peace, hope, and joy. The term *heart* has many uses in Scripture, but its basic meaning refers to the deepest core of the person. The heart is the fundamental, yet sometimes hidden, fountain at the deepest recesses and absolute center of a person from which spring one's genuine, real feelings, one's most authentic thoughts, one's actual values and take on life. In this sense, it is obvious that the heart is the deepest aspect of one's soul, one's inner self, and it is not to be equated with the organ that pumps blood.

But in chapter 1, we saw that the soul is fully present throughout the body and that one's body parts can actually contain, or be associated with, sinful or holy tendencies to act, think, and feel in certain ways. In my view, it is no accident that the term *heart* is used to represent one's deepest core, for the physical heart area—what C. S. Lewis called "the chest"[10]—is the "location" where we actually experience our deepest values, feelings, attitudes, and ways of seeing the world. In some mysterious way, then, the physical heart area, especially what is going on there, is to be the center of meditation if it is to flow from and impact our deepest core, our metaphorical "heart." And when one is experiencing anxiety/depression, one needs to get to the core of what is going on.

Attending to the physical heart muscle is an application

of two important biblically based theological themes. First, we are to ask God to search and know us, especially any hurtful ways in us (Psalm 139:23–24). But it would be sub-Christian to colabor with God in searching only the mind. We are holistic bodies and souls, so our focusing, our attention, our "searching" with God, should include inviting the Holy Spirit to help us do body scans to see if there are any emotions or other sensations in our bodies that have significance to us and to God's desire for us to mature in Christ.

Second, we are to present the members (e.g., organs, body parts) of our bodies to God as instruments of righteousness (Romans 6:12–13, 19). There are many ways to do this, but one is to submit different members to God's searching gaze and go there with him to see what he wants to show us about ourselves. And outside of the brain, the organ of the physical heart may be the most important member of our bodies to present to God's searching and our own colaboring with him in this. So when one is doing a body scan, one is following a biblically based practice.

A third strand of thought—a scientific one—derived from recent discoveries may shed light on biblical teaching about the core of a person and its relationship to the heart organ. Neuroscientists have discovered that the heart has its own independent nervous system, referred to as "the brain in the heart." In a real sense, the heart "thinks for itself." Some forty thousand neurons are in the heart, which are as many as are found in a number of important subregions of the brain.

The heart sends signals to different parts of the brain,

including the amygdala. The amygdala specializes in strong emotional memories and is what the soul uses to process information for its emotional significance. By influencing the amygdala and other regions of the brain, scientists believe that "our heartbeats aren't just the mechanical throbs of a diligent pump, but an *intelligent language* that significantly influences how we perceive and react to the world."[11] Some scientists talk about "heart intelligence," an intelligent flow of awareness and insight, an intuitive source of wisdom and clear perception that embraces both mental and emotional intelligence.

In biblical terms, the soul is the person, but the soul has two faculties of intellectual cognition and intuitive perception, and each is associated with a different body part—the brain and the heart, respectively. Thus, the brain and the heart work together to shape our thoughts, emotions, moods, and attitudes. Given that a person is a single self—not two—with one soul, it is obvious that the "I," the soul, uses both the mind (associated with the brain) and the deepest intuitive core (associated with the heart organ) to think about, intuit, and feel the world.

In light of the new scientific information, one can only marvel at the incredible accuracy of Paul's statement: "Do not be anxious about anything, but in every situation, by prayer and petition, with thanksgiving, present your requests to God. And the peace of God, which transcends all understanding, will guard your *hearts and minds* in Christ Jesus (Philippians 4:6–7, emphasis added). Note carefully that the context is one of feeling anxiety. Given this context, we learn that both the heart and mind areas of the body (the heart organ and the brain) are to be involved cooperatively in opening up to God and dispelling anxiety.

With this in mind (and hopefully in your heart!), I want to explain a practical technique for meditatively handling anxiety and depression, *especially obsessive thoughts* that one does not have the power to set aside. This technique was first presented by stress researcher Doc Childre and is adapted here to take into account both the biblical teaching on the two strands mentioned earlier in the chapter and my own practice of this form of meditation.[12]

Note first that when one is anxious or depressed, one tends to obsess, to think over and over again, about certain fearful or hurtful thoughts. We do this to try to anticipate a bad or worst-case scenario and to reassure ourselves that we are safe, that we can handle it. We also relive traumatic events and their associated emotions; we replay our depressive, anxious fears and thoughts and their associated emotions. Sometimes we do this for a thought or emotion that we *can* handle. We can't face all of our fears and worries, so we sometimes project all of them onto one or two issues that are "safer" for us to dwell on.

In the early stages of my 2003 anxiety-induced depression, while I had suffered a number of different stressors in ten months, I began to think over and over again about two of them. This let me set aside the remaining stressors and try to manage my anxiety with a more limited, "controllable" focus. The problem with this strategy is that one gets into a rut that becomes increasingly hard to escape from. Indeed, studies have shown that obsessive thought and emotional patterns and behaviors literally create a neural pathway, a groove in the brain, that becomes habitual and contributes to a situation in which a person is literally stuck on a pattern, stuck in a rut.

Among other things, this means that trying to battle anxiety and depression in the head by obsessive worrying is a losing battle. After a while, if one tries to keep from repetitively entertaining the worry, one has to exert considerable energy inward to suppress the worry, which can deplete the brain of needed chemicals and lead to anxiety/depression. And as a reward for all the effort, one simply digs a deeper groove associated with the worrisome thought that makes it harder to get off one's mind.

Rather than battle anxiety and depression in the head, I recommend a different four-step meditative strategy to deal with it *in the heart*. This strategy is a life-enhancing form of meditation all throughout life—with or without anxiety/depression—but, at least for me, it is especially useful to form it as a habit during a season of obsessive mental suffering.

I will describe the HeartMath Solution exercises below and in chapter 6. Before proceeding, however, I want to be clear about two things so as not to create confusion about my own use of these exercises to draw near to God and grow in character and emotional health. First, some statements that have been made on behalf of the HeartMath Solution have been extreme, weird, and, in my view, unsubstantiated. For example, some have claimed that the heart's electromagnetic field has been measured up to 100 meters distance from one's body; others claim that changes in people's collective emotions, including those caused by changes in the heart muscle, affect the earth's geomagnetic field and ionosphere! Some researchers have questions about various applications of the HeartMath Solution theory.[13] I distance myself from all these claims, and, in fact, here and in chapter 6, I am affirming the usefulness in my own life and in those of others I know of the exercises and only the exercises I use in this book.

Second, when someone teaches a text properly, they have a "Thus saith the Lord" authority in what they are saying. But when someone offers suggestions about how to apply a biblical text to one's life, they do not have biblical authority in what they are offering. Rather, one is providing some suggestions that may be helpful in applying that text to one's life. We have been exhorted by Scripture to present habitually different "members" (e.g., body parts, organs) to God as instruments of righteousness, shalom, peace, flourishing. The specific HeartMath Solution exercises I'm suggesting are my attempt to provide you with something to try as a way to present your heart muscle to God. I am offering a way of applying biblical commands that many have found helpful. My employment of specific exercises is nothing more than that. That said, here is the four-step exercise.

Obsessive Thoughts and the Four-Step HeartMath Solution
STEP 1: *Freeze-Frame*

When obsessing on an anxious thought or stressful feeling, *freeze-frame it*. Take a time-out. If you have an anxious thought or stressful feeling right now, recognize it and bring it before your mind. Suppose it is the fear of financial ruin. As this thought and its associated emotion run over and over again in your awareness, freeze it—that is, stop your mental engine from running over and over again, and like stopping a film projector, stop in mid-thought and freeze it. Step 1 helps a person to obey the biblical injunction to cease striving and stop fretting (see Psalm 46:10; Philippians 4:6). If it helps, you can tell the thought that you will get back to it in a short while.

STEP 2: *Refocus*

With all your might, *shift your focus* away from your racing mind or troublesome emotions and focus the center of your attention on your physical heart muscle. Attend to the center of your chest where your heart is and stay there for about ten to sixty seconds. The goal is to feel the area around your heart. Many people erroneously think that the heart muscle is on the left side of the chest. But this is wrong. Actually, the heart is located between the two lungs in the middle of the chest slightly toward the left of the breastbone (or sternum), which is at the front center of the chest.

There are three ways to help you in this. First, pretend you are breathing in and out of your heart muscle. Second, place your hand over your heart to help draw your attention to that area. Third, try to "feel" and attend to the front surface of your physical heart, then to the back surface, followed by the right and then the left side of your heart. When first learning to practice this meditative activity and form it as a habit, you can take as long as necessary to focus on the heart area. My first attempt required about thirty minutes before I could keep my mind from darting around and I could stay focused on my heart muscle.

At this point, you may feel little emotion there or you may get in touch with a feeling of embarrassment, fear, grief, sadness, loneliness, helplessness, hurt, or some other anxiety producer. Step 2 is an aid in internalizing Proverbs 3:5: "Trust in the LORD with all your heart and lean not on your own understanding." Rather than mulling things over and over again in your mind and trying to solve your worries in the head, turn to the core of your inner life—your heart—and learn to trust God there. Remember, the physical heart is a window into the spiritual heart, the very center of who you are. Step 2 is a way to practice not leaning on your own understanding. Step 3 is a way of learning to trust God *in the heart.*

STEP 3: *Wait for the Emotion*

Using the acrostic CFAN (**C**ompassion/Care, **F**orgiveness, **A**ppreciation, and **N**onjudgmentalism), recall a memory that involved some relevant, positive emotion to be mentioned shortly. *Stay with the memory* until the associated emotion can be felt in the heart muscle. Then let that emotion dwell in and dominate the heart area. The goal is not to recall the memory but to have its associated emotion be felt in the heart. With your attention on your physical heart area, you want to bring a new positive emotion, a healthy intuitive awareness, to dwell there and replace the feelings already there from the worrisome thought you have frozen. To do this, you want to meditate on something positive in order to recall a memory emotion that is positive. You want to recall a specific occasion in which you gave or received *compassion* (love)/care, *forgiveness*/removal of guilt feelings, *appreciation*/joy, or *nonjudgmentalism*/acceptance.

The important thing is not to try to do all four of these, but to pick one that is most effective for you and constantly return there. For example, recall a time when you gave real love to God, a friend, or a family member or received love from God or someone important to you. Recall a time when you expressed appreciation to someone—a special time of worship when you really felt God was there or a time when you gave heartfelt praise and adoration to someone—or a time when you drank in appreciation from the taste of a good cup of coffee or from a spectacular answer to prayer or an endearing biblical truth.

Many people have found it helpful to picture a person or situation—a child, a friend, a pet, a place of peace or love, a positive action done to you. Once the picturing brings about the relevant feelings in the heart area, let the picture image go and focus your attention on the feelings in the physical heart. The goal here is not simply to recall—as you are picturing it—the relevant incident, but more importantly, to *have the associated emotion fill and remain in your heart area.* If you are unable to feel the emotion, say, of appreciation, then adopt the attitude of appreciation.

STEP 4: *Melt the Anxious Thought*

While holding this emotion in your physical heart area, return to the anxious thought and melt it piece by piece into the heart area, and with full sincerity ask your heart, "Next time, what would be a less stressful, less anxious, more effective response to this thought and the situation to which it refers?" Listen to the heart area for an answer.

The goal of step 4 is to so trust in the Lord with your whole heart that you form the habit of responding there to a specific worry with feelings of compassion, forgiveness, appreciation, or a nonjudgmental attitude toward yourself or others, as well as with a new perception—a fresh, positive perspective on the situation in particular and on life in general. Each situation in our lives is an occasion for either positive formation or negative deformation. The HeartMath practice may increasingly help one respond to life's situations *in a positive, formative way*. As Doc Childre and Deborah Rozman remind us, "While everyone experiences stress, what you do with it makes the difference in how much happiness and contentment you experience."[14]

This is what I mean by breaking down the worrisome issue into pieces and melting it into the heart: Take the thought, for example, that you are going to be ruined financially, and break it down to its parts ("My children will be embarrassed at school by their clothes; I will be out of a job; my family will look down on me"). By taking that part to the heart area, you allow the anxious thought (e.g., "I will be out of a job") to be overwhelmed by and newly associated with the positive emotion already in the heart area and not with negative ones.

If done at various times each day, a habit will be formed that will allow you to set aside an obsessive thought and not be stuck on it. In the process of setting the thought aside, it will allow you to be able to entertain it without being overwhelmed by negative emotions. In my experience, one can literally learn to have the thought while feeling, say, joy and compassion. I invite you to experiment with this in order to learn by repeated practice to overwhelm obsessive thoughts with the positive emotions present in the heart area rather than battling the obsessive thought with more thoughts in your head.

Now, while your heart is not a separate person from you, we all talk to ourselves throughout the day. Indeed, depending on the nature of our self-talk, it is an important aspect either of a healthy or a dysfunctional Christian life. So as part of step 4, in dependence on the Holy Spirit (see Psalm 139:23–24), you can ask your physical heart area (literally address the area of emotion surrounding the heart as a form of self-talk) about a better way to respond, and you can look for a mild intuitive insight that comes from the heart area. Generally, the insight will not shout at you; it will be a soft, mild thought or feeling that can be easily overlooked if you are not attending to the heart area.

Summary Thoughts about the HeartMath Solution

Experts recommend that a person do various HeartMath practices, especially the four-step one I've just described, three times a day for five minutes each or ten times a day for a minute each.[15] By repeating this four-step form of meditation at different times each day, I've been able to train myself to lead a more mature, stable Christian life and to set aside anxiety/depression. It may help you to get unstuck from negative thinking and emotional patterns too—especially anxious and worrisome habits—and to replace them with positive thoughts and feelings of warmth, safety, and happiness.

BULLET-POINT SUMMARY

- Anxiety is largely a habit wired or grooved into the brain and nervous system.
- Replacing old thinking habits with new thinking habits through certain daily practices helps to get rid of anxiety.
- How we think largely affects how we feel.
- Our self-talk goes largely unnoticed, and with the aid of the Holy Spirit, we must learn to notice it more regularly.
- The Four-Step Solution can be practiced several times a day: relabel, reframe, refocus, revalue.
- We need to identify our most frequently used distorted thinking traps.
- Focusing requires getting into a flow.
- We should avoid ruminating about negative self-talk.
- The HeartMath Solution can deal effectively with obsessive thoughts one cannot get out of one's mind by direct effort.
- We don't need to battle obsessive thoughts in our mind. Instead, we can disempower them in our heart region.

Chapter 4

Spiritual and Psychological Tools for Defeating Anxiety/ Depression:

Part 2

Those of us who suffer from anxiety and depression want to get rid of these enemies. They rob us of so much life and productivity. And that is not just my opinion. The Scriptures—especially the book of Proverbs—contain several sober acknowledgments about the contrasting results in one's life from having a cheerful, peace heart versus a defeated, anxious, depressed heart.

Proverbs 17:22 reads, "A cheerful heart is good medicine, but a crushed spirit dries up the bones [i.e., saps a person's strength]." Those of us who have had our fair share of anxiety know how true this statement is. Anxiety "dries up the bones" faster than a marathon run in August through Death Valley! If you try to fight anxiety head-on, it can drain you of energy and make you listless. And perhaps the worst thing about anxiety is being anxious about getting anxious and losing hope that things will ever be different. I've been there, and I never want to go back.

But therein lies the rub. What, exactly, can you do to make it unlikely that significant anxiety returns? Look at the first part of Proverbs 17:22 again: "A cheerful heart is good medicine." We all know that. And it is widely known that a heart full of joy, peace, and happiness is extremely valuable when it comes to good physical (and mental) health. But are these just words, perhaps words to incorporate into a worship song? Our problem is not with believing the truth of this statement.

Indeed, when we read these words, they spark a longing, a hunger in our hearts to have this for ourselves. But how do we get this? Is it really possible for our lives to be steadily characterized by a joyful heart? Can peace and joy be our default setting emotionally?

In the last chapter, I provided information about two habit-forming practices that, in the span of a few months, replaced for me anxiety-producing negative thoughts and self-talk with their healthy counterparts. These two practices were among a short list of five to six things that changed my life, a fact to which my family and close friends will readily attest. In this chapter, I will describe two additional practices from my short list. If you will engage in these practices every day until they and the emotions they produce become ingrained in your body and mind as habits, I believe you may be able to replace the anxiety default position with a peace and joy default position, especially if these practices are done as part of an overall plan of care under the supervision of a therapist.

What are these two disciplines? They are the practice of *contemplative prayer* and the regular expression of *gratitude*.

THE DAILY HABIT-FORMING PRACTICE OF CONTEMPLATIVE PRAYER

MY DISCOVERY OF CONTEMPLATIVE PRAYER

Regarding contemplative prayer, Dr. Susan Muto has observed, "It attunes me to the presence of God in a space out of which flows God's participation in my daily life and from which I avoid distractions and sins. It is foundational to Christian character formation as it stills the heart; guards my soul; liberates from evil thoughts, words, and actions; focuses on divine grace; and evokes the power of the life of Jesus in me, which bears the fruit of virtues and overcomes vices that provoke my soul."[1]

I have found Muto's reflections to be true in my own life. I have practiced contemplative prayer for two hours a day (one hour early in the morning and one hour in bed before my normal time to drop off to sleep) for two and a half to three years.[2] I mention this to say two things: (1) I was desperate to get rid of anxiety once and for all if possible, and contemplative prayer was one of the ways I sought to do that; and (2) practicing this sort of prayer each day proved to be absolutely central in my quest to replace anxiety with the peace and joy that contemplative prayer can achieve for many practitioners. One does not need to practice contemplative prayer anywhere near two hours a day to benefit greatly from it.

I love to pray, and I suspect you do too. Shortly after I became a Jesus follower in 1968, my mentor Bob Farnsley taught me the widely used acronym for prayer called ACTS—Adoration, Confession, Thanksgiving, and Supplication—which is a wonderful tool for recalling and performing various aspects of prayer. Indeed, ACTS constituted my understanding of prayer for the next few decades of my Christian life. However, as I began to grow in Christ, I longed for more, and I started reading spiritual formation literature for help. In that literature, I found a gold mine of teaching, practices, and resources for drawing near to God and being transformed in a healthy, Christ-honoring way.

As I continued to read, I learned about a different form and purpose for prayer than the ones captured by ACTS. That form was contemplative prayer, so about two and a half years ago or so, I added it to my use of ACTS and thus both broadened and deepened my prayer life. There are two purposes for contemplative prayer as a spiritual discipline: (1) to attach emotionally and intimately to our loving God—to love God with all our hearts, to seek God for his own sake, even if we do not experience something; and (2) to transform our character by learning to center and calm ourselves, to focus without distraction on a member of the Trinity or on God in general (whichever approach helps you the most), and to see anxiety depart and be replaced by peace and joy.

Regarding the second purpose, I have some good news! According to journalist and author Rob Moll, twelve minutes of this sort of attentive, focused prayer each day for eight weeks can change the bad grooves in the brain (e.g., the anxiety-triggering grooves) enough for the change to be detected on a brain scan.[3] Prayer that changes our brains and replaces anxiety with peace and joy requires deep, fully focused openness to and concentration on God.

My Practice of Contemplative Prayer: Steps 1–5

There are many different ways to practice contemplative prayer. I will share the approach I use, but feel free to tweak it to suit your own needs. The important thing is that your employment of contemplative prayer works and helps you fulfill increasingly the two purposes listed above.

Step 1

Find a comfortable, quiet, private place you can regularly use. It may be helpful to get ear plugs to enhance your sense of quiet. Some people find it helpful to set a timer for whatever length of time you plan to be in prayer. That way you don't have to keep looking at the clock if your schedule is tight, which can be very distracting.

Step 2

Spend a few minutes relaxing your body and mind. Do a brief body scan to see if there is any particular place in your body that is tense or anxious or feels different than usual. Pay special attention to three locations: your brain, your heart muscle, and the places where you typically manifest stress.

In appendix 1, I have included a number of "encouraging verses." Dallas Willard once told me he found it helpful to have four or five verses committed to memory to which he would turn regularly each day. These verses, he said, came to form the very rails on which he lived his life. I suggest you do the same. The verses you select should be ones that thrill, comfort, and encourage your heart when you hear or think about them. In the appendix, I have listed several of my favorite verses. You may find four or five there that you would like to memorize and treat as ones that help form your core self.

I use my verses, or at least some of them, during my period of contemplative prayer. Recall that we are at step 2, where we have relaxed, scanned our body, and found a tense or otherwise distracting feeling. Mine usually occurs in my head, so at this time, I place my hands on my head and pray, "Peace I give you," or, "Be at peace." I direct this prayer at the distracting place in my body. These different prayers are based on John 14:27 (see appendix). I imagine the Spirit letting peace flow from his presence within me through my hands into my brain and head area. I then speak the Lord's peace to my entire being, using part or all of John 14:27.

Step 3

I tell Jesus that I come to him as a fallen, needy, broken, wounded person who needs him and his warm, loving presence. I often use 1 Peter 5:6–7 ("Humble yourselves, therefore, under God's mighty hand, that he may lift you up in due time. Cast all your anxiety on him because he cares for you.") as I do this. When I say "humble yourselves, therefore, under God's mighty hand," I follow this with "Father, I am humbled by my brokenness and neediness. I bring nothing but my broken self." After "that he may lift you up in due time," I acknowledge that my flourishing, my escape from anxiety, and so forth is in his hands and that I desire to cooperate with him and wait on his help and presence.

After "cast all your anxiety on him because he cares for you," I am careful not to use this as a time to obsess on all the sources of anxiety in my life. That would take away from the purpose of contemplative prayer. Rather, I will express two or three of my main worries and tell the Lord, "These are just too much for me to handle. I cannot face or carry them on my own. So I let go of them now and release them to you, along with all my other unspoken fears, so they will not get in the way of us connecting in intimacy. This is our time to connect, and our time alone. With your help, I will let nothing distract me from seeking you."

I follow this with Proverbs 3:5–6 ("Trust in the LORD with all your heart and lean not on your own understanding; in all your ways submit to him, and he will make your paths straight."). This reinforces my confidence in God to carry my anxiety during the time of contemplative prayer, and it keeps me from ruminating on my problems.

Step 4

I am now in an open, calm, receptive place. It is time to open my heart to God and love him from my heart, to seek to connect with him, and to put myself in a place of waiting and anticipation for the Lord to make himself real to me or speak to me if he chooses. I express my need to cling to him with my whole being. By the way, many times, nothing discernible happens after this, so I simply wait calmly and patiently in God's presence. I know he is right there before me, even if I'm not experiencing his presence. As I wait, I seek to maintain my gaze on God, being aware that he maintains his gaze on me, whether or not I experience it. I have found two verses especially helpful to use at the beginning of this time of opening my heart to God. I use one or the other sometimes, and I also use them both if I sense the need:

- "Thou wilt keep him in perfect peace, whose mind is stayed on thee: because he trusteth in thee" (Isaiah 26:3 KJV).

- "Let go and relax, and experience me as God" (Psalm 46:10, my paraphrase). What is it that you let go of? Your entire life. This is the time to say again, "God, I let go of my whole life for a while. I give my mind, heart, and body permission to relax, and I seek to experience your presence."

Step 5

During the entire time of contemplative prayer, but especially during step 4 as you enter a time of quiet waiting, seeking, and longing, it is very easy to get distracted. If you find your mind wandering, don't beat yourself up. Gently let go of a distracting thought or simply let it pass by as you would a wave while swimming in the ocean. Don't stuff or resist the thought. Then gently bring your focus back to God by quietly repeating a biblical word or simple phrase like, "Jesus." "Abba, Papa." "I receive you." "Jesus, have mercy on me." "Peace." "I love you dearly." If these aren't helpful, find your own. The point of repeating these words or simple phrases is to draw your distracted focus back on God and your openness to him. Once that is restored, you no longer need to recite your word or phrase.

It may also be very useful to picture helpful things in your mind. For example, you may try to imagine Jesus coming over to where you are praying, standing before you, and reaching out his hand to hold yours. Or when you place your hand on an anxious place you discovered during your body scan and you begin to pray or speak peace to that area, imagine Jesus' hands on top of yours, colaboring with you to speak peace to the problematic body area. Sit quietly and be open to God, but don't try to make something happen. If you don't sense God's presence, be content with the knowledge that you quieted your heart, sought after him, and sat calmly and patiently before his presence for a period of time.

FIVE REFLECTIONS ON CONTEMPLATIVE PRAYER

I offer a few reflections that I hope will help you in your practice of contemplative prayer as you pursue your victory over anxiety.

First, start this discipline by taking ten to fifteen minutes each day to engage in contemplative prayer. If possible, do it at the same time each day so it's easier for it to become a habit. Don't get discouraged if you miss a day or two. Just recommit to this formative practice and go from there.

Second, anything worth learning—playing tennis, speaking Spanish, crocheting—is awkward, unnatural, frustrating, and hard to do in the early stages of learning. You will fail repeatedly and hit the tennis ball into the net on a regular basis! But if you form the intention to stay at it, you will become better and better at what you are learning. Nowhere is this more evident than learning to engage in contemplative prayer, especially if you gradually seek over time to increase your engagement to, say, thirty minutes a day.

When I started, I regularly got distracted, I could not focus on the Lord for very long, and I got very little out of the practice. So what else is new? This is just the way it is when learning something new. Still, the emotions associated with these thoughts and actions are very destructive and false, so stay at it! In my case, I began to see real, experiential improvement after about two months of daily practice, and in my experience, two to five months is what it will take for this to become second nature. You will start doing it automatically, and, in fact, if you miss a day, you will long to get back to it, just like joggers feel if they miss a day. If you want to replace anxiety with peace and joy, I've found that this is one of a handful of habit-forming practices that work.

Third, Dallas Willard used to say that the last thing on your mind as you drift off to sleep will tend to occupy your subconscious attention through the night. In this way, it will have a formative impact on you for good or bad, and it will usually determine your mood when you wake up the next morning. So he would take the minutes between getting into bed and falling asleep to calm his heart, think about Jesus (e.g., imagine him standing next to you, picture a scene from the Gospels, gently meditate on a biblical passage on your list of encouraging verses), and express his affection and longing for God.

I have done this for two and a half years as of this writing, and it not only helps me drift off to sleep, but it also brings me closer to God and has the effect Dallas Willard noted. Through practice, you too can form the habit of refusing to ruminate on your worries or anxiety triggers, and as you seek to drift off to sleep, you can set aside thinking about what you have to do tomorrow. If you need to, before you go to bed, write these things down on a piece of paper and forget about them. If something you forgot to write down comes to mind while you are trying to practice Willard's advice, ask yourself which is more important—making sure you remember the new responsibility or learning to stay calmly focused on Jesus?

Fourth, if you fall asleep during your time of contemplative prayer, when you wake up, express gratitude to God for it. Not only have you not "failed" somehow; in reality, your body is telling you something and you responded appropriately. Most likely, either you're not getting enough sleep or the sleep you're getting is not deep enough. The Centers for Disease Control and Prevention did a study in 2009 in which "35.3 percent of Americans reported that they typically got less than seven hours of sleep daily."[4]

Sleep deprivation is bad for your mental and physical health, and it is a factor in obesity, diabetes, high blood pressure, and a weakened immune system. It also has a highly negative effect on anxiety and other mood disorders by impacting one's brain chemistry in such a way that it makes one more vulnerable to such disorders. Many experts say that one needs between seven to nine hours of sleep each night. I am in the nine-hour range, and if I don't get close to nine hours of sleep for a few days, I can sense that my mood changes. So the last thing you want to do if you fall asleep during contemplative prayer is to beat yourself up, feel guilty, and call yourself a failure. Instead, give thanks for the nap and, if necessary, pick a different time of the day to engage in contemplative prayer.

Fifth, and finally, I must address the negative reaction of a minority of evangelicals to the sort of contemplative prayer I and millions of other Christians down through the centuries have found so life-giving. The concern is that contemplative prayer involves imagination/imagery and the use of a repetitive mantra. Both are thought to be unbiblical and, in fact, since they are used in New Age practices, should be avoided at all costs by biblically faithful Christians.

Let me address the issue of *imagination and imagery* first. For one thing, imagery that fires the imagination is all throughout the Bible. Read the book of Ezekiel or the opening of the book of Revelation and see for yourself.

Second, when God the Son became incarnate, God the Father took the "risk" of having people who lived while Jesus walked on the earth use their memory-image of what he looked like. And when these people got greater clarity about the deity of Jesus, they most likely used their memory-image of him in worship and prayer after he was resurrected. If God was concerned with imagery and imagination in approaching him, that concern would have counted against the incarnation, but we have no biblical record that God the Father ever gave this a second thought.

Third, imagery and sense perception put us in touch with beauty, as the history of art has demonstrated, especially Christian art. Millions of Jesus followers have been strengthened in their faith through Christian art of this sort. Dallas Willard said that beauty warms and opens the heart to goodness (e.g., to receiving and obeying biblical teaching). And he once said that no one could be angry while looking intently at a lush garden full of beautiful roses!

Finally, this negative reaction is based on a failure to understand properly the role of an image in acts of thought and feeling. Let me explain. Suppose you want to think about London for as long as you can. And you would like this period of thought to bring to your mind warm feelings for the British people. If you simply try to think about London in the abstract with no imagery in mind, you will be easily distracted and not stay focused on London for very long. But if you conjure up an image, say, of the Tower of London, the image will allow you to concentrate on London for a much longer period of time.

This is one reason Bible memory work is enhanced by repeating the verses out loud or looking at them on a card as you try to memorize them. In each case, sensory imagery (through sound or vision) helps us focus longer on the verses than we can without them. Return to the London example. You neither think about your image of the Tower of London (you're thinking instead about the Tower of London itself), nor do you think with your image (you think with your thoughts and direct them toward London). So what role does the image of the Tower of London play? It is a sensory image in your consciousness that helps you keep your focus on London for a longer period of time. That's all it does.

If I picture Jesus standing before me or use some other

image in contemplative prayer, I am neither focusing my attention on the image nor using the image to focus my attention on Jesus. Rather, I am focusing *on Jesus himself* and using my thoughts and intentions to do so, and the image is merely a tool to keep me from getting distracted. This is why such imagery employed in contemplative prayer does not violate the second commandment: "You shall not make for yourself an image in the form of anything in heaven above or on the earth beneath or in the waters below" (Exodus 20:4).

If misunderstood, this commandment would rule out art altogether, and that is absurd. As the context just before and after this commandment makes crystal clear, the concern here is to refrain from creating a finite, sense-perceptible object for the purpose of directing our attention on it to worship it. But as we have seen, in using an image to pray, one neither directs one's attention on the image nor uses the image to direct one's attention on something else. The image is a tool to increase the duration of one's ability to focus on God.

What about the objection to the use of a mantra (repeating words such as "Jesus," "Abba," and so forth) in the practice of contemplative prayer? Isn't this a New Age or even Buddhist practice? Not at all. For one thing, in many non-Christian religious practices, a mantra is a word, syllable, or sound that need not have syntactical structure or any literal meaning at all. When chanted, many practitioners think the resultant melodic structure is resonant with various supernatural or otherworldly qualities. Further, it is the mantra itself that is the focus of the chanter's attention.

But none of this is true of the use of "Jesus" or "Abba" in contemplative prayer. All the words I recommended above are pregnant with deep Christian meaning and significance. Moreover, no one should think that repeating these words all by themselves puts one in touch with a set of supernatural, otherworldly qualities. The focus of attention is not on the word itself. Rather, the repetition of a word like "Jesus" is done to bring one's focus back on Jesus or on the entire Godhead. The purpose of repeating a special word or phrase is to get us to the point that we won't need to do this any longer, either in a prayer session in the early stages of learning or when we are months into contemplative prayer. The hope is that we will get to a point where the "training wheels"—the words or phrases—are no longer needed.

While Jesus does warn us to avoid the use of meaningless repetition in our prayers (see Matthew 6:7), this exhortation has nothing to do with the repetition of deeply meaningful words in contemplative prayer. Right after the warning, Jesus gave his followers a prayer to memorize and repeat—the Lord's Prayer. Clearly, Jesus was not against repetition.

Furthermore, if I were to tell you to avoid eating the spoiled food in the refrigerator by using the qualifying word *spoiled*, it becomes clear that I am not telling you to avoid the food in the fridge; I am warning you against a specific kind of food there, namely, the spoiled food. Similarly, Jesus is warning against meaningless repetition, not against repetition per se. And what sort of meaningless repetition did Jesus have in mind? In the same verse, he makes the answer to this question very clear: "Do not keep on babbling like pagans, for they think they will be heard because of their many words." This repetition is a form of works-righteousness—if I simply pray long enough and repeatedly, this will form the basis for God listening to me. The contrast with contemplative prayer should be evident.

I want to conclude my response to this negative critique with two general points that I believe are at the heart of the criticisms. First, something can be unbiblical by being antibiblical (e.g., adultery) or extrabiblical (e.g., the use of an organ in worship, having small groups in one's church). There are two attitudes one can adopt toward the Bible and truths or helpful practices outside the Bible. One can say that if something is not in the Bible, it is forbidden. There is no biblical basis for this attitude, and if we adopted it, no pastor could give his own thoughts about the practical application of a passage because those ideas would not be in the Bible.

Alternatively, one can say that if something is not in the Bible, we are free to believe or use it as long as (1) there are reasons to believe it is true, and (2) there are reasons to believe it will help me in my Christian growth and love for God. This second approach is far more sensible, and there is no biblical case against it. This approach, then, forbids antibiblical teaching and practice but is willing to consider on a case-by-case basis the acceptance and use of extrabiblical ideas. Obviously, I accept the second approach and, accordingly, embrace contemplative prayer.

My second general point may require a bit of thinking.

In logic, there is a form of reasoning that is proper. It is called *modus ponens*, and this form of reasoning guarantees that if the premises of an argument are true, then the conclusion must be true. Here is an example: (1) If it is raining outside, then it is wet outside. (2) It is raining outside. Therefore, (3) it is wet outside. If (1) and (2) are true, then (3) has to be true.

But there is a mistaken and rationally dangerous form of reasoning sometimes associated and confused with *modus ponens*. It is the fallacy of *affirming the consequent*. Here is an example of this fallacy: (1) If it is raining outside, then it is wet outside. (2) It is wet outside (here we affirm the truth of the consequent of (1). Therefore, (3) it is raining outside. But (3) does not follow from (1) and (2). It could be wet because a fire truck hosed down the neighborhood; everyone had their lawn sprinklers on at the same time; or a tsunami hit the area.

What in the world does this have to do with the negative reaction to contemplative prayer? Simply this: The negative reaction is an example of affirming the consequent. Consider the following fallacious argument: (1) If Howard is a New Age practitioner or advocate, then Howard uses imagery and repetitive words or phrases. (2) Howard uses imagery and repetitive words or phrases. (This affirms the consequent.) Therefore, (3) Howard is a New Age practitioner or advocate. But this is clearly wrong. Others may use imagery and repetitive words or phrases too. This becomes evident if we examine the following counterexample: (4) If Howard is a New Age practitioner or advocate, then Howard breathes, eats food, seeks to lead a good life, and fasts. (5) Howard breathes, eats food, seeks to lead a good life, and fasts. Therefore, (6) Howard is a New Age practitioner or advocate. But all kinds of people, including atheists and Christians, breathe, eat food, seek to lead a good life, and fast. This does not make them New Age practitioners or advocates. Similarly, for centuries upon centuries, Christians have used imagery and repetitive words and phrases in contemplative prayer to change their lives and draw close to God. Throughout most of this time, there was no New Age movement yet. This kind of critical reaction to contemplative prayer is based on a fallacy.

THE DAILY HABIT-FORMING PRACTICE OF EXPRESSING GRATITUDE TO GOD

In recent years, psychologists working in the "positive psychology" school of thought have made a commonsense yet exciting discovery: Cultivating a disposition of gratefulness through daily practice will produce a deeply ingrained habit of seeing the world half full (or even more!) instead of half empty. Perhaps the leading authority on the study of gratitude is UC Davis professor Robert Emmons. Emmons, a deeply committed Christian, makes this rather stunning observation:

> Gratitude has one of the strongest links to mental health and satisfaction with life of any personality trait—more so than even optimism, hope, or compassion. Grateful people experience higher levels of positive emotions such as joy, enthusiasm, love, happiness, and optimism, and

gratitude as a discipline protects us from the destructive impulses of envy, resentment, greed, and bitterness.[5]

Gratitude or thankfulness is the heartfelt acknowledgment that I have received a good gift, that I recognize the value of the gift and know that at least part of the source of this gift lies outside of me, and that I express my appreciation to the donor for his good intentions toward me. Thus, gratitude involves acknowledging, recognizing, and appreciating. Gratitude is other-directed. One can be grateful to God or other people, but not to oneself. Gratitude both helps us and requires a willingness to set aside "the negativity bias"—the habit of seeing and feeling the world in a grumpy way—and replacing it with a positive outlook on life, indeed, with a positive worldview in light of which we see, feel, and think about the world.

According to Emmons, dozens of research studies have demonstrated that we can do something about our anxiety and happiness, and expressions of gratitude are at the core of what we can do in dependence on God's Spirit. Here are some of the benefits of the regular practice of gratitude:[6]

- increased feelings of energy, alertness, enthusiasm, and vigor
- success in achieving personal goals
- better coping with stress
- a sense of closure in traumatic memories
- bolstered feelings of self-worth and self-confidence
- solidified and secure social relationships

- generosity and helpfulness
- prolonging of the enjoyment produced by pleasurable experiences
- improved cardiac health through increases in vagal tone
- greater sense of purpose and resilience

Wow, what a list! If we're not careful, we may even come to think we were designed to flourish best when we are thankful and grateful! Yet as exciting as these psychological studies are, we didn't need them to know the importance and value of expressing gratitude and thanksgiving to God. The Bible insists on this. It is filled to overflowing with exhortations to be grateful to God and express thanksgiving to him. For example, "For everything God created is good, and nothing is to be rejected if it is received with thanksgiving" (1 Timothy 4:4). Or consider this: "Let us come before him with thanksgiving and extol him with music and song" (Psalm 95:2).

It is important to get to the place where we see everything that comes into our lives, especially difficult things like panic attacks or intense periods of anxiety, as an occasion for formation and growth or deformation and decline. How we label things makes a big difference in our emotional life. But we all know that the formation response is not easy to achieve. We all have things in our lives that are obstacles to gratitude: a habitual tendency to be negative and to worry, an inability to acknowledge dependency on others, internal psychological conflicts, making comparisons with others we perceive to be more fortunate, taking on a victim mentality, or having a history of suffering. By relying on God, we can engage in the position exercises regularly so that, over time, the formation response is grooved into our character. We may grow to see life as a continual invitation to gratitude. And it is important to keep in mind that gratitude is not primarily a feeling. Rather, fundamentally, it is a stance one takes, a positive approach to life.

How, then, does one cultivate a grateful way of seeing life? The answer is by practicing the expression of gratitude at different times each day until thanksgiving becomes second nature. While it does take time, when done faithfully, I was able to see progress in a few months.

There are at least three ways to practice gratitude as a spiritual discipline: regular, daily expressions of gratitude; keeping a gratitude journal; and writing gratitude letters.

The first way is fairly obvious: expressing gratitude for a handful of specific things at different times of the day. However, a few observations may help you to practice this more effectively, especially as a way of defeating anxiety. First, you may not feel grateful or want to express gratitude to God. Perhaps you're thinking, *Isn't it phony and hypocritical to go ahead and express gratitude in these circumstances?* Maybe, if you have no interest in growing in real gratitude. But even if you don't want to express gratitude, if all you can muster is to want to want to, then that is all you need to avoid hypocrisy. Why? Because you really want to get to the point where you regularly and genuinely feel grateful and want to express it, and you know that forming a new habit requires doing things you may not want to do in the early stages of formation. Just do it, and the feeling and sense of gratitude will come in due season.

Second, express gratitude for things you really are grateful for and not for things you are supposed to feel grateful for. Among other things, this means the alleged "small, insignificant things" are not truly small or insignificant. They should be part of our daily expressions of thanksgiving. I regularly get up in the morning and start by expressing my gratitude for coffee, for my easy chair, or for whatever I'm truly grateful for.

Finally, Robert Emmons notes that research has identified four important facets of gratitude: intensity, frequency, span, and density.[7] *Intensity* refers to a person with a strong grateful disposition who just experienced a positive event. One would expect this person to respond with intense gratitude. By way of practical application, be on the lookout for things in your life you are intensely grateful for, and be sure to include these items in your daily practice. Also, as time goes on, be aware of how your gratitude intensity is growing.

Frequency refers to how often you feel grateful each day. As you grow, more and more things in your life should spark gratitude. *Span* refers to the number of life circumstances for which a person is grateful at a given time. As your gratitude span grows, you see more and more of your life as holding occasions for gratitude. Finally, *density* refers to the number of people to whom one feels grateful for a single positive outcome or life circumstance.

There are two payoffs for knowing these four aspects of gratitude. First, it gives us eyes to see and evaluate how different aspects of gratitude are growing in our lives rather than simply attending to the general notion of gratitude to assess growth. In fact, one or two aspects of gratitude may be growing but another may not, and this can provide helpful information for self-reflection, sharing with friends, or mapping a strategy for growth in the slower-moving aspect. Second, it gives us a way to meditate on our lives so we can engage in different aspects of gratitude. We may decide to focus on one aspect and not another. What matters most is that we experiment with all this to see what works best for us individually.

The second way to practice gratitude as a spiritual discipline is daily to write down in a gratitude journal the things for which you are grateful that day. Here you remind yourself of the gifts, grace, benefits, and good things you enjoy. We often use journaling to write down our daily pains, sorrows, and fears. But a gratitude journal has a very different purpose—the cultivation of the ability to notice the good things in one's day and not the bad ones.

Finally, another way to practice gratitude as a spiritual discipline is monthly to write a gratitude letter to someone and visit them so you can read them the letter. Think of people who have made a difference in your life and for whom you are really grateful. Pick one and write a letter to that person—a page or two is best—listing all the things about that person you're grateful for. If he or she lives close enough, call them and say you would like to come over for a few minutes and share with them something that will encourage them. Then visit the person, tell him or her what you've done, and simply read the letter to the person. I have done this, and the shared joy is tremendous and edifying. If the person lives too far away for a visit, you can read your letter to them over the phone.

The bottom line is that the cultivation of the habit of expressing gratitude to other people—but especially to God—changes your life and, among other things, can reduce anxiety. In the last two chapters, I have presented four practices that have saved my life. I cannot overstate their impact on me. My prayer is that they may be helpful to you as well as you seek life-giving change that makes your anxiety a thing of the past. But it would be irresponsible if I left things here, because more specific interventions involving my brain and body have also been part of my healing. I will turn to those interventions in the next chapters.

BULLET-POINT SUMMARY

- Anxiety affects physical health.
- Daily habit-forming practices can replace anxiety brain or body grooves and habits with peace and joy body or brain grooves and habits.
- Daily engagement in contemplative prayer for at least twelve minutes can change brain structure.
- You can learn and practice your own adaptation of the five steps of contemplative prayer listed in this chapter.
- Negative criticisms of contemplative prayer fail to be convincing.
- Of all personality traits, gratitude has one of the strongest links to mental health and satisfaction.

- How we label things makes a big difference in our emotional lives.
- The habit of expressing gratitude turns one from seeing a glass half empty to seeing it half full.
- We can all express gratitude a few times daily for a handful of things we are really grateful for, including the "little" things.
- Four important aspects of gratitude are intensity, frequency, span, and density.
- Some find it helpful to write daily in a gratitude journal.
- I encourage you to write and deliver a gratitude letter once a month.

Chapter 5

BRAIN AND HEART TOOLS FOR DEFEATING ANXIETY/DEPRESSION

Early in the morning on Sunday, October 5, 2003, my wife, Hope, and I boarded a plane for Baltimore. Two of our dearest friends, Jim and Jeanie Duncan, were living in the Baltimore area. Each had spent their entire lives in New England, New York, and Maryland, so they knew that part of the country like the back of their hands. For eight months, the Duncans had labored to prepare a spectacular weeklong trip for the four of us, exploring historical sites, gazing at the fall leaves, staying in bed-and-breakfast inns, and enjoying food, drink, and fellowship. It was the trip of a lifetime.

But not for me. On May 23 of that year, I had been blindsided with my first clinically severe panic attack, and, unknown to me at the time, I would continue in a deep "nervous breakdown" until the day after Christmas of that year. All of this was new to me, and I was having trouble understanding what was going on. Since I was on sabbatical that fall, I had nine months to follow my own schedule and build as much rest into it as I needed. About two weeks into my breakdown, I started weekly therapy—a process that would last for five years—with a wonderful Christian therapist.

I had no idea then of the crucial biological aspects in my brain and body—especially my heart muscle—that were contributing to my anxiety disorder. In addition, I knew nothing about antianxiety/antidepressant medications. To be honest, I had a bad attitude toward this sort of medication.

For one thing, I was scared. I was afraid it would make me feel drugged, increase my dysfunctionality, and cause side effects that just wouldn't be worth it.

Plus, I was afraid of what being on that medication would say about me. Without medication, I was able to lie to myself with self-assuring self-talk that I really wasn't that sick, and in any case, my problems would soon be over. But taking medication would be serious business, and it would mean I was much sicker than I told myself (which was, of course, the real truth). Medication would make me face my condition, and it generated anxiety about getting anxious once again. Besides, I was a mature Christian leader. Surely I wasn't so weak that I needed meds! This was a spiritual and emotional issue that could be solved just by reading the Bible, attending church, and so on. I had overlooked the fact that I had a body and a brain, and that as a holistic person made in God's image, every aspect of me affected every other aspect (see chapter 1).

I now realize I was a complete idiot. I was self-deceived and woefully ignorant about how to treat and heal from anxiety and about how medication could help. But after two months of getting worse, even though I was reading the Bible, praying, and going to therapy, I finally listened to a good friend, swallowed my pride, and went to my primary care physician. Often, a primary care physician is qualified to prescribe antidepressant/antianxiety medications, though a specialist in these medications—a psychiatrist—is often the best choice. In my case, I began to take the medication and dosage my physician prescribed, but by the time our New England trip came along, I was not getting better.

For most of the trip, I was dysfunctional and anxious about everything, and I spent a lot of time in bed. The trip was ruined for me, but, thank God, the other three were able to enjoy the trip while caring for me at the same time. One evening, I had such a severe panic attack that I called my therapist's emergency phone number, and we talked for about ten minutes, even though he was in the middle of a birthday party for his daughter. I had a prescription of Xanax in my possession, but I had been afraid to take it. So he urged me to do just that, and it helped, but I was too afraid to do what I needed to do—to take it every day while we were on the trip. After taking that one pill, I went back to my withdrawn state.

At that time, I received a word that would change my life. One of our friends on the trip told me if my primary care physician's approach to my medication was not working, I should see a psychiatrist. I followed her advice. At my first visit to a psychiatrist, she increased my dosage. With the aid of medication, therapy, and spiritual practices (though I wouldn't learn about the practices I've shared in this book until ten years later), I began to get better. While it took two to three weeks for the increased medication to take effect, it was clearly the missing ingredient. It was so effective that in two months—the day after Christmas—my anxiety abruptly left. I began to feel normal again. I had forgotten what that felt like and had been afraid I'd never feel that way again.

This was my introduction into the importance of the brain in treating anxiety. In earlier chapters I shared the spiritual and psychological aids that can indirectly affect the brain in a positive, antianxiety way. In this chapter, I will discuss tools that can directly affect the brain.

THE BRAIN AND ANXIETY/DEPRESSION

MEDICATIONS

I am not a medical doctor or a psychiatrist. If you want to know more about medications, I have listed good books in the appendixes that explain how antianxiety and antidepressant medications work.[1] I do know of the tremendous value of such medications, at least for me. Prescription medications are so effective today that, with rare exceptions, few people any longer need to suffer from severe anxiety and depression. To be sure, they do not work well for everyone, and they can have some undesirable side effects; a health care professional can guide you in this area if you believe you would benefit from medication.

But we Christians often have an irrational, unbiblical aversion to taking these medications. There can be a terrible stigma associated with them. I've already mentioned my experience when I was a guest preacher at a church. After the first service, the elders told me their church doesn't believe in such medications, that I had spread false teaching, and that I was to leave out reference to medications in my second message. A few days after this experience, I got an email from the senior pastor, who had been gone the Sunday I had preached. He told me as soon as my first message was over, his cell phone was barraged with texts from congregants expressing their horror at what I had said. He scolded me and offered me pastoral counseling, and I haven't been invited back to that church in the last twelve years.

I have spoken on two hundred college campuses and have had things thrown at me, have been shouted down in the middle of talks, and have been booed when I preach the gospel. I wasn't hurt personally by the incident at the church. But I was saddened by the ignorance of the pastor and leaders of the church. Who can calculate the unintentional harm they may have been doing to people in the congregation who needed medical help to cope with anxiety or depression. Almost certainly a number of congregants that day were on such medications, but unfortunately, they couldn't make it known or they would face being socially ostracized.

This kind of negative, stigmatizing attitude toward anti-anxiety/antidepressant medications is unbiblical and violates common sense. It is unbiblical for three reasons. First, as I explored in chapter 1, biblical anthropology is functionally holistic. That is, it teaches that the various aspects of a human person—the mind, emotions, body, soul, spirit, will, and so forth—all affect each other in complicated ways. Among other things, this implies there will be a bodily component to spiritual or psychological problems, and to tackle those problems, a person will need to address all the affected aspects of himself or herself, including the brain.

Second, teaching on spiritual disciplines follows Romans 6:12–13, 19; Romans 12:1; Colossians 3:5; and other texts in affirming that fleshly and harmful habits are stored in the various members of our bodies in the form of grooves, and the brain is one such member. Helping the brain get well by using all available tools, including medications, is both biblical and sensible.

Finally, the apostle Paul recommended to Timothy not to drink water exclusively, but also to have a little wine to help with his stomach and other ailments (1 Timothy 5:23). The water was not always good to drink in those days, and wine was regularly taken as medication. It is no accident that archaeologists have discovered that the fields of Israel in Jesus' day were filled with grape vineyards. What we don't realize, however, is that in several places, the Bible recommended the use of alcohol in those days as a medication to deal with anxiety and depression and to stimulate joy, happiness, and celebration (see Deuteronomy 14:26; Proverbs 1:6–7; Ecclesiastes 2:3; 2:24; 3:13; John 2:1–11).

By no means do I want to offend you by mentioning these verses, especially if you believe that the Bible teaches abstinence regarding alcohol or if you are an alcoholic who cannot stop after one sip. If you disagree with what I have said, I hope and pray we can agree to disagree civilly and continue our search together for help in minimizing or getting rid of anxiety. My main point is simply that the Bible recommends the medication available at the time for psychological and spiritual issues. To be clear, I would never suggest to someone that they try to deal with anxiety or depression only by taking medications. Instead, I would urge that they attack the problem holistically and use physical (including medical), spiritual, and psychological tools to get better. While medications have been crucial for my own restoration, at the end of the day, they are not for everyone. But at the very least, a Christian can and should be open to exploring this option without shame or feeling like a spiritual failure.

Some hold the idea, "I can be strong and spiritually mature enough to rely on the Lord alone to solve my anxiety issues without turning to medications." Besides, they may continue, "I don't want others to disrespect me for having to turn to medications." Without being mean-spirited, these may be the lamest excuses I've ever heard. Do any of us "rely on the Lord alone" for headaches, skin cancer, diarrhea, a broken leg, or a severely abscessed tooth? No, we pray and take medicine and go to the doctor.

Why should it be any different with anxiety? After all, while it is not only a brain issue, it is surely in part a brain issue. For whatever reason, our brains can reach the point where they are no longer able to produce the chemicals (e.g., serotonin) needed to sustain positive feelings and moods and avoid negative ones. It has helped me to regard antianxiety/antidepressant medications as vitamins for the brain. They supply what the brain is not currently able to.

Of course, before anyone considers taking medications, they should consult with a certified doctor and place themselves under his or her care. A primary care physician or a specialist in medications—a psychiatrist—can accurately diagnose the situation, share the potential side effects of taking such medications, and prescribe (or not prescribe) what is best. Most people I know who are on these medications, and there are many, say the side effects aren't bad, and the medications, once they've gotten used to them, do not make them feel drugged or abnormal. If you are prescribed medication, it is important to remember that if the initial prescription doesn't work well, you should tell your doctor what isn't working and what you are experiencing. It may take time to find just the right medications, or the current medication may require more time to take effect. In my experience, though, under the proper medical care, you can rest assured that you will be guided in a way that is best for your individual case.

Some people claim that nonprescription remedies are better than prescription antianxiety/antidepressant medications, and besides, one simply cannot trust the drug companies. But in my opinion, these ideas are false. Remember, "natural" remedies come from a fallen world and aren't necessarily "natural" in the way God originally intended. After the fall, there is a lot in the natural world that is not natural (i.e., good; the way God created it to be). And medications have been subjected to rigorous testing for effectiveness and dosage, while "natural" remedies are tested, if at all, in a much less rigorous way, and there is seldom careful research regarding dosage. As in so many areas of medicine, medically developed treatments are far better than home remedies.

As for trusting drug companies, we don't generally apply

such suspicion to other companies. We buy clothing, computers, household goods, lawnmowers, and hosts of other things made by companies whose primary goal is to make money. Like almost all companies in a capitalist society, the drug companies want to increase their profits. But they face competition in the market that encourages them not to sell harmful or ineffective medications. Mistakes are made in all industries, but in general, I believe the medications developed by drug companies are helpful, especially because of the rigorous testing to which they are submitted.

I close this section on antianxiety/antidepressant medications with an observation. If you are hurting severely, it is hard to get on with normal life, including practices in your Christian life. If you have intense stomach cramps, painful arthritis, or some other significant pain, you simply cannot concentrate until the pain is treated. This is exactly what millions of us have found when it comes to medication and getting rid of anxiety. I will stake my reputation on the effectiveness of the ideas I shared in earlier chapters for my own recovery. But when my anxiety was severe, I simply could not stay focused enough to engage in those ideas and practices in a helpful way. I needed to address the intense anxiety. For me, medications made that possible. While I continued to pray and go to therapy, it took about a month until the medications lowered my anxiety to a level at which I could really dive in and focus intensely on the habit-forming practices listed in earlier chapters. And many other sufferers have found this to be the case as well.

EMDR (Eye Movement Desensitization and Reprocessing) Therapy and Bilateral Stimulation

Talk therapy is a very helpful tool for dealing with anxiety, especially when combined with the other tools already discussed. Indeed, during and after my first nervous breakdown beginning in May 2003, I began a five-year journey of talk therapy with a good Christian therapist. We would talk, and he would make observations, give me direction, and provide a safe place for me to explore my past and present issues. Finally, we reached a point when both of us agreed it was time to stop.

When I had my second nervous breakdown in 2013, I didn't want to do talk therapy again. I had virtually gone off medication at the time, so I upped my dosage with my psychiatrist's help, and after doing hundreds and hundreds of hours of research into the various aspects of anxiety, I developed new strategies—the ones I'm sharing in this book—that have launched me into a new place of calm and joy in my life, a place I hadn't experienced before in more than sixty years of living.

I became aware of a tool that was being used by numerous Christian and non-Christian therapists with great effect in curing anxiety (especially PTSD, panic attacks, stress, and painful and anxiety-producing memories) and depression. It was a new form of therapy, at least to me, that numerous studies showed to be effective. Before I describe it, I should mention that more research is being done on EMDR therapy, and it is a mode of treatment that is not accepted by all psychiatrists. Furthermore, it is not meant to be a replacement for talk therapy but a supplement to it. In my case, EMDR yielded solid benefits in my healing. It is unknown to many Christians and could be worth researching if you think it might help you.

I want to demonstrate how biblical EMDR is by rehearsing some of what I've mentioned in earlier chapters. You may recall that music is not literally on a CD. Rather, there are digitalized grooves such that if the CD is not damaged and is placed in the right retrieval system (e.g., a CD player), then the grooves are triggered and music occurs in the surrounding room.

Similarly, memories and consciousness generally are not in the brain (when your soul leaves your body at death, your memories go with you because they reside in the soul and can exist without a brain). Rather, while we are in the body, events—especially traumatic ones—create grooves in the brain that, when triggered, bring about a memory in the soul (as long as the brain is not damaged and you are "scanning" your past, trying to access the memory). When Psalm 139:23–24 urges us to invite God to search us and know us, especially any anxious thoughts we may have, the invitation applies to all of our aspects—the body and all its members, along with the soul and all its faculties (e.g., mental, volitional, emotional faculties). During this process, we should colabor with God as he directs us.

Part of the search can involve the brain and its memory-triggering grooves. During my six months of EMDR therapy with a wonderful Christian therapist, it was remarkable how much it helped me. Why? EMDR involves a technique discovered almost by chance in 1987 that helps get to isolated, painful memories whose brain grooves are so deep and isolated that ordinary talk therapy may not reach them. In fact, during my EMDR therapy, I experienced memories I hadn't recalled in more than sixty years, and when I did, I was able to connect them with other memories, feel and acknowledge the events recalled, release them, and integrate the memories with the rest of my life.

Think of it this way. If a wound gets infected and closes itself off from the rest of the body, it will not heal. What is needed is for the wound to be opened so the blood and immune system can have access to it and integrate it with the healthy parts of the body surrounding the wound. In the same way, some traumatic memories are associated with brain grooves that are so deep and isolated that they do not get opened to heal, and they may unconsciously contribute to our anxiety, especially to panic attacks, and we have no idea this is happening. In my experience, EMDR was able to reach those deep and isolated grooves, open them up and expose them, and integrate them with the rest of the mind and brain. In this way, EMDR can be seen as one form of practical application of Psalm 139:23–24.

On the website of the EMDR International Association, here is its response to the frequently asked question "How does EMDR work?"

No one knows how any form of psychotherapy works neurobiologically or in the brain. However, we do know that when a person is very upset, their brain cannot process information as it does ordinarily. One moment becomes "frozen in time," and remembering a trauma may feel as bad as going through it the first time because the images, sounds, smells, and feelings haven't changed. Such memories have a lasting negative effect that interferes with the way a person sees the world and the way they relate to other people.

EMDR seems to have a direct effect on the way that the brain processes information. Normal information processing is resumed, so following a successful EMDR session, a person no longer relives the images, sounds, and feelings when the event is brought to mind. You still remember what happened, but it is less upsetting. Many types of therapy have similar goals. However, EMDR appears to be similar to what occurs naturally during dreaming or REM (rapid eye movement) sleep. Therefore, EMDR can be thought of as a physiologically based therapy that helps a person see disturbing material in a new and less distressing way.[2]

EMDR facilitates rapid eye movement so one experiences what is called bilateral stimulation. Bilateral stimulation is the goal, and it involves undergoing a left-right rhythmic pattern that activates the left hemisphere of the brain and then the right hemisphere, and back and forth for a period of time. Believe it or not, this is understood to "loosen up" one's brain grooves and release traumatic memories so healing can occur. It is the bilateral stimulation that does the work, and rapid eye movement is simply one effective way to bring about that stimulation. Other ways can be effective as well, such as sitting in a comfortable chair and tapping one shoulder and then the other, back and forth, or one thigh and then the other.

In a therapy session, an EMDR therapist may have you hold your head steady and ask you to follow his or her hand with your eyes (without moving your head) as he or she moves it back and forth for anywhere from a minute to five or more minutes. You are then asked what, if anything, you are recalling, experiencing, or feeling. If appropriate, this process may go on for the entire session.

EMDR may also be done at home by oneself. One of the world's leading experts on EMDR, Dr. Laurel Parnell, has developed an approach to do it alone in a life-transforming way (especially as a tool to replace anxiety with peace, calm, and joy).[3] As she mentions in a disclaimer on the copyright page, anyone who practices this technique should first consult with a licensed qualified therapist, physician, or other competent professional.

Parnell's employment of EMDR is not aimed at surfacing negative or traumatic memories, experiences, or emotions. That should be done in the presence of a trained therapist. Rather, she has adapted EMDR to bring out the reservoir of positive stored experiences within us that stimulate a positive mood.

Her adaptation is also useful for putting more deeply and permanently positive images and other helpful resources into our souls and brains that we can learn to access. If a person begins to find fearful or overwhelming emotions surfacing, they should stop EMDR practice and see a trained therapist. Here are Parnell's steps for practicing EMDR by oneself.

First, after finding a comfortable place and closing one's eyes, imagine or picture a positive resource. For example, bring to mind a memory of when the resource was experienced, an image that evokes it, or a person who embodies or represents it. The resource may be something like peace, joy, love, power, and so on. I would choose something that counteracts anxiety. The more detail that is brought to the imagination, the greater the effect it will have.

Parnell instructs that we try to feel the resource (e.g., the image, the memory, the representative person's presence). When this is accomplished (I might feel calm, joyful, and so on as I imagine the resource), tap it in by tapping six to twelve times, using right-left, right-left on the shoulders or thighs. This roots the resource and emotion more deeply into one's being.

According to Parnell, there are four major things to tap in: (1) a safe, peaceful place; (2) images of nurturing figures (images of Jesus are especially effective for me; I also use my memories of Dallas Willard); (3) images of protectors; and (4) figures who provide inner wisdom.[4] A person could also tap in a quality needed to cope better, such as courage.

Parnell suggests that a person tap in at a time when they are not in a situation of immediate need, with the exception of a time of need when they can apply an already tapped-in resource to a current situation. She notes that this form of tapping in is especially effective for healing anxiety.

If you are interested in EMDR, you can visit www .biolateral.com; I've personally benefited from "The Best of BioLateral II/BioLateral CD #6," which includes some of the most soothing music I have ever listened to going back and forth between the left ear and the right ear.

In sum, I highly recommend considering EMDR therapy as an aid in the battle against anxiety or depression. If you are interested, I urge you to consult an appropriate professional. I also recommend from personal experience the tapping-in technique found in Parnell's book.

THE BODY: THE HEARTMATH SOLUTION ONE MORE TIME

As we begin this section, it will be helpful to take a brief look again at the current stress epidemic and its impact on all of us. Doc Childre, who is the founder of HeartMath, and his colleague Deborah Rozman, who is its president and CEO, wrote this about stress:

> [Here is] a malady of modern times: unremitting and increasing levels of stress. The statistics on mounting stress and its detrimental effects on body, mind, emotions, and health shout at us. The American Institute of Stress notes that 75 to 90 percent of visits to primary care physicians are for stress-related complaints . . . A Harvard study shows that people who live in a state of high anxiety are four and a half times more likely to

suffer sudden cardiac death than nonanxious individuals . . . An international investigation reveals that people who are unable to effectively manage their stress have a 40 percent higher death rate than their nonstressed counterparts.[5]

When stress becomes a habit mentally, emotionally, and physically, a default setting on our inner dial, then it becomes "normal" and we no longer notice its presence. But the stress is still there, and it affects how we perceive, feel, and react to events in our lives. And stress is the major cause of anxiety.

So how do we get rid of stress? Interestingly, scientific studies have demonstrated that changing our heart rhythms is more effective at alleviating stress than techniques like relaxation.[6] According to Childre and Rozman, "You can release a lot of stress by going straight to the feelings underlying it, then regulating your emotions and heart rhythms . . . When you go to your heart and find a new rhythm, you often find a new perception or solution that makes the situation less overwhelming, and the stress goes away."[7] And they further claim there is good news because "exciting new research on the heart has found that there is a way to relieve stress that both comforts you and—most importantly—transforms stress into healthy positive feelings and creative energy."[8]

In chapter 3, I explained the HeartMath technique for getting rid of obsessive, anxiety-producing thoughts. In this section, I will introduce a broader use of HeartMath ideas and techniques that can apply to one's life in general. The holistic applicability of HeartMath tools is just what a Christian would expect, given the centrality of the heart in Scripture.

The Bible presents two different notions of *heart*. First, there is the more spiritual and soulish notion according to which the heart is the center or seat of one's emotional, intellectual, volitional, spiritual, and moral faculties. When *heart* is used of a specific aspect of the person, say, the emotions, it refers to that aspect in its deepest, and often most hidden, facet. Thus, when we say, "Let's get to the heart of the matter," we mean we should stop focusing on surface issues and get down to the real, underlying issue. Again, when we say, "I love you from the bottom of my heart," we mean to emphasize we love from our very depths.

Moreover, the "spiritual and soulish heart" was taken by the ancients to be a faculty of intuitive perception, a way of sensing right and wrong, a tool for spiritual perception, a vehicle for being aware of the emotional state of another person or group. As the apostle Paul put it, "I pray that the eyes of your *heart* may be enlightened" (Ephesians 1:18, emphasis added).

Why do the Scriptures use the term *heart* to refer to this component of intuitive awareness; of centering our mind, emotions, and so forth; and of being at the very depth of our lives? The recent renewed emphasis on spiritual disciplines has brought certain texts (e.g., Romans 6:12–13, 19) into more careful focus and provides us with the answer. Emotions and other conscious states reside in certain members (organs, regions) of our embodied souls. Understanding this, the ancients believed—quite correctly—that these spiritual and soulish aspects of *heart* were embodied in, or at least deeply correlated with, the heart muscle.

Interestingly, modern scientific research seems to have validated what the biblical writers and the ancients knew all along. According to Childre and Rozman, "The heart brain takes an active role in communicating with the head brain, sending more signals to the head than it receives in return . . . Scientific evidence indicates that intuitive information is received first by the heart; then it's sent to the brain (head)."[9] Elsewhere, they note that the body, primarily the heart, picks up on another's feelings through a sort of emotional, intuitive perception, whether or not the mind is conscious of it.[10]

It's important to recognize that the spiritual and soulish heart is not another component or faculty of the person alongside the others (the mind, the emotions, the will, the spirit). Rather, *heart* is a way of talking about these components in their deeper aspects. For example, when the Scriptures say, "For as he thinketh in his heart, so is he" (Proverbs 23:7 KJV), I believe this text refers to the deepest aspect of the mind. So it could be translated, "For as he thinketh in the deepest core of his mind, so is he."

Consider this illustration: Suppose we have on a table four water glasses and we name them "the mind glass," "the emotions glass," "the will glass," and "the spirit glass." Now suppose we fill the glasses two-thirds full of water and then pour into each a third of a glass of a dark heavy fluid. This fluid sinks to the bottom and creates a clear boundary between the dark fluid gathered in the lower third of each glass and the water in the upper two-thirds of each glass. If we chose to use "the dark glass" to describe our situation, this term would not refer to a fifth water glass. Perhaps somewhat awkwardly, "the dark glass" would refer to the deepest area of the four glasses. "The dark glass" provides an analogy with *heart*, a term that does not refer to a different component; rather, it refers to the other components in their deepest aspect.

Second, besides the "spiritual and soulish heart," the term *heart* is used for an organ in the body between the two lungs, near the center of the chest, slightly to the left of one's breastbone. For a long time, Christians have tended to separate the two uses of *heart*, and that is appropriate in some contexts. But the following point is so important that it bears repeating: As I mentioned in chapter 1, the renewed emphasis on spiritual disciplines has returned to center stage the habitual practice of engaging the members (organs, bodily regions) of the body as a means of psychological or spiritual transformation.

Thus, it makes sense to see many of the "spiritual and soulish" scriptural teachings about the heart as having a direct correlation with transforming, habitual presentations of the heart organ to God as instruments of righteousness. This brings about flourishing or shalom and, in turn, the reduction or even elimination of anxiety.

Two aspects of the heart organ are especially important for achieving and retaining positive emotional health and ridding one's life of anxiety, depression, and other negative emotions: heart rhythm and the heart's electromagnetic field. Regarding heart rhythm (beat-to-beat heart changes or variability), by studying electrocardiograms (ECGs), scientists have discovered a critical link between emotional states and rhythms of the heart. If a person is experiencing positive, uplifting emotions (e.g., appreciation, care, compassion, love), this creates a smooth, rhythmic heart pattern shown on the ECG. Childre and Rozman call this pattern a coherence waveform.[11] By contrast, people who are feeling negative emotions such as anxiety created jagged, disordered heart rhythms called incoherent waveforms. Learning how to achieve coherence—a coherent waveform—in the heart will help replace anxiety with positive emotions of appreciation, love, care, safety, and so on.

Regarding the heart's electromagnetic field, scientists have discovered that there is a measurable electromagnetic field surrounding every person. It is a combination of the electromagnetic fields generated by the brain, the heart, and other electric systems in the body. According to Childre and Rozman, "The heart's electromagnetic field has forty to sixty times more amplitude [roughly the size of the field's oscillations—an indicator of the field's strength] than that of the brain, while the heart's magnetic field is approximately five thousand times stronger [has more intensity] than the field produced by the brain."[12] The heart's field has been measured at least ten feet from the heart muscle, and this is one reason a person's emotional state can be picked up and internalized by another person within a range of ten feet or more. The field changes with different internal emotions, e.g., with differing stress levels, and as the field changes, it communicates different "messages" to the brain, triggering positive or negative thoughts.

What does all this have to do with victory over anxiety? Simply this: The heart organ—especially its rhythmic coherence or incoherence and the nature of its electromagnetic field—is directly connected to one's emotional state. By learning to work with the heart muscle—presenting it to God as an instrument of well-being—we can achieve longer and longer periods of positive emotion and learn how to get rid of anxiety if or when it surfaces.

The heart muscle is one of the most important (if not *the* most important) organs that contributes to emotional, spiritual, and psychological health or sickness. As Proverbs 14:31 reminds us, "A heart at peace gives life to the body." Similarly, Proverbs 17:22 notes, "A cheerful heart is good medicine." On the other hand, Proverbs 15:13 (NASB) warns us that "when the heart is sad, the spirit is broken." Finally, Proverbs 12:25 observes, "Anxiety weighs down the heart."

HeartMath tools are practical ways to engage the heart muscle in this way. Before I present two HeartMath exercises that have worked well for me, I want to note two points of perspective: (1) These exercises are useful commodities with documented effectiveness over anxiety, but they are effective only if practiced appropriately and regularly, ideally as part of a daily routine; and (2) learning to perform these exercises well is like learning anything new—they will be hard, feel unnatural, and may not be helpful in the earlier stages of learning how to do them, but with regular practice, the more helpful these exercises can become.

PRACTICE #1: QUICK COHERENCE

This simple exercise is a powerful way to refocus emotion and reconnect with the heart muscle to release stress, balance emotions, replace anxiety with appreciation or peace, and feel better quickly. It takes only a minute or so to perform the technique, and it has helped me to feel at ease and peaceful. Here is how it works.[13]

STEP 1: HEART FOCUS. Focus attention on the heart. If you have difficulty with this, try wiggling your big toe and focus on it. Then focus on one of your elbows. Finally, focus on the center of your chest—the heart area. It may help to put your hand over your heart muscle. If your mind wanders, gently bring your focus back to your heart.

STEP 2: HEART BREATHING. While focusing on your heart muscle, imagine that you are breathing in and out of the heart area. Breathe in slowly and gently through your heart (Childre and Rozman suggest to a count of five or six), and do the same in breathing out. Scientific research shows that this sort of breathing synchronizes your breathing and heart rhythm and starts to bring coherence to the heart's rhythm. Do this until your breathing feels natural, smooth, and balanced. Keep doing this until you achieve an inner rhythm that feels good to you. This will take longer when you are first learning the practice.

STEP 3: HEART FEELING. As you continue to imagine breathing through your heart (this allows you to stay aware of the heart area), recall a positive memory associated with a positive feeling (appreciation works best for me, as does a feeling of calm and security, but other feelings such as being joyful, being forgiven, and being cared for and loved also work). This memory can involve anything that is not immoral—an event involving a special person, a pet, an accomplishment, a fun activity, a victory for your favorite sports team, or a special place you like. Once the positive feeling is there, continue your breathing and focus on the feeling in the heart area. If you don't feel anything, then simply adopt a sincere attitude of appreciation, care, and so forth. This can be done, for example, by praying silently or softly out loud words that express or engender the attitude (e.g., "I am safe and peaceful now"; "I so appreciate my home").

Quick Coherence shifts our focus from thoughts—our mind and our brain—to emotions and the heart. In first learning this tool, I found that it took me five to ten minutes to perform because I had difficulty bringing the memory-associated emotion into focus in my heart. In any case, once practiced for several weeks, this technique should only take a minute or two. It can be done five to ten times a day, or it can be performed anytime it is needed, such as in the middle of or right after a tense situation.

This and other HeartMath exercises have been especially effective for me in dealing with anxiety. Studies have shown that people can change, even if their anxiety is a long-standing habitual trait, by using HeartMath tools.[14] So there is hope, even for those who have had a serious anxiety problem for a long time. I can testify to this personally.

PRACTICE #2: HEART LOCK-IN TECHNIQUE

This practice is similar to Quick Coherence, but its purpose is to help internalize positive emotions into a habitual, emotional default position. The first three steps are virtually the same as those in Quick Coherence, but step 4 is the key difference.

- Step 1: Focus attention on your heart muscle or the area around it.
- Step 2: Imagine you are breathing in through your heart (for a count of five or six) and out through your solar plexus (located four inches below the heart).
- Step 3: Activate a genuine feeling of appreciation, care, and so forth (e.g., toward someone or something in your life).
- Step 4: Make a sincere effort to sustain feelings of appreciation, care, and so forth while directing them toward yourself or others.
- Step 5: When you catch your mind wandering, gently refocus on your heart and your breathing and then on the positive emotion located there.

Childre and Rozman recommend practicing this exercise in a quiet place for five to fifteen minutes one or more times a day. They also suggest doing it when first waking up or before going to sleep at night. I have been doing it two times a day, both morning and evening, for about two and a half years, and it has been invaluable. One tip: the mind tends to ruminate throughout the night on the last items thought about before going to sleep, which is one reason it is so emotionally helpful to do this exercise in bed before drifting off.

Up to this point in the book, I have sought to tell the story of my own journey with anxiety, provide a sketch of a functionally holistic view of the human person, and share what I have personally found to be effective approaches to minimizing or getting rid of anxiety and depression. These approaches include spiritual, psychological, and physical tools. I have tried to zero in on things that may be less known about anxiety and that were of most help to me. I have intentionally left unmentioned a number of factors that are important but widely known, such as getting rest and exercise and developing friendships. If you would like more information on anxiety and depression and how to best address them, I have included in appendix 4 an extensive list of recommended reading that may provide you with additional help.

In the next chapter, I want to conclude these reflections on anxiety by offering my understanding of key biblical themes that I've found particularly helpful in my own journey.

BULLET-POINT SUMMARY

- See a primary care physician or a psychiatrist for advice on antianxiety/antidepressant medications suitable for your specific situation.
- Antianxiety/antidepressant medications are so good today that few people need to suffer from severe anxiety

or depression. But they don't work for everyone, and they can have side effects.

- Taking medications for negative psychological feelings or moods is biblically based.

- Antianxiety/antidepressant medications can be fruitfully depicted as vitamins for the brain that supply what the brain is currently not able to provide for itself.

- In general, and for many people, prescription medications for anxiety and depression are more effective than "natural" remedies.

- Medications lower the intensity of anxiety/depression so spiritual/psychological practices can be utilized more effectively.

- In my experience, it's best not to address anxiety/depression with medications alone, but to be holistic and also use spiritual and psychological tools.

- EMDR therapy can be an effective supplement to talk therapy for releasing the power of isolated and deeply lodged painful feelings and memories. What has worked well for me is tapping in (1) a safe, peaceful place; (2) images of nurturing figures; (3) images of protectors; (4) figures who provide inner wisdom. Qualities necessary for better coping, such as courage, can also be tapped in.

- The HeartMath exercises of Quick Coherence and the Heart Lock-In Technique are most effective if practiced regularly.

Chapter 6

Suffering, Healing, and Disappointment with God

YOU ARE AND FEEL WHAT YOU THINK
(ESPECIALLY ABOUT GOD)

Neuroscientist/psychiatrist Daniel Amen and neuropsychiatrist Lisa Routh remind us that "what you allow to occupy your mind will sooner or later determine your feelings, your speech and your actions. Thoughts . . . have a real impact on how you feel and behave."[1] This truth has become a major theme in my understanding of anxiety.

UCLA neuroscientist Jeffrey Schwartz has done experiments in which people's brains are monitored as they watch videos of carnage at automobile accident scenes. The anxiety center of the brain goes wild. Then he tells them to pretend they are paramedics who must make snap decisions about whom to treat first and what to do. When showed the same scenes, the anxiety center remained calm. One can alter one's brain and its role in facilitating anxiety, depression, and so forth by changing how one thinks and adjusting one's perspective. Here was Schwartz's punch line: People who see the glass half full regarding their lives are healthier, happier, and more functional than those who don't. And, he said, Christian theists who have a background belief, a worldview that God is real, good, and caring, will have a substantial leg up on those who don't have such a belief.

The bottom line: We are what we think. Even better,

we are what we believe, because studies show that to change our brain chemistry, defeat anxiety and depression, and have a pervasive sense of well-being, it is crucial that we spot the false ways we think about life and replace them with thoughts we take to be true. As psychologists Edmund Bourne and Lorna Garano remind us, "The truth is that *it's what we say to ourselves* [the self-talk of our thought life] *in response to any particular situation that mainly determines our mood and feelings.*"[2]

In 1979, Christopher Lasch's bestseller *The Culture of Narcissism* appeared on the scene. It remains one of the most insightful analyses of American culture I have ever read. Lasch analyzed cultural patterns during the previous twenty-one years, and the book's subtitle was grim: *American Life in an Age of Diminished Expectations.* According to Lasch, beginning around 1958, therapists began to face an escalation of patients who did not suffer from any specific problem. Instead, they suffered from vague, ill-defined anxiety/depression that seemed "to signify an underlying change in the organization of personality, from what has been called inner-direction to narcissism."[3]

Something had gone wrong with the American psyche itself, which had become numb with pervasive feelings of emptiness and a deep fracture in self-esteem. More and more Americans were preoccupied with their own self-absorbed, infantile needs, along with the instant gratification of desire. As a result, they found it impossible to form intimate relationships with others and to live for something bigger than they were, to identify with some historical stream (for example, the outworking of the kingdom of God or the progression of American ideals and values) that gave meaning to their lives and with respect to which they could play a role.

Here is Lasch's concluding description of the narcissistic personality ubiquitous in our culture: "The ideology of [narcissistic] personal growth, superficially optimistic, radiates a profound despair and resignation. It is the faith of those without faith."[4] In referring to "those without faith," Lasch is talking about the rise of secularism, along with the religious skepticism, cynicism, and indifference that go with it. And secularism is responsible for the "profound despair and resignation" that lie in the subconscious bosom of many of us.

We are fed secular ways of thinking at our mothers' knees; we are socialized into a naturalistic and atheistic (or agnostic) way of seeing the world. It is the very air we breathe. Some time ago, the *New York Times* published an article claiming that the difference between Europe and America is that Europe embraces secularism and America embraces religion.[5] The article recommends that America follow in Europe's steps. Secularizing factors such as this pelt us daily, and they are so widespread and frequent that they are hardly noticed.

Indeed, it is its stealth nature that explains how secularization gets past our defenses and forms the deepest part of the American psyche, even for religious believers. My graduate students from Africa, South America, and Asia tell me they regularly see miracles of healing (including blind or lame people made well through prayer) in their services. They are befuddled at the weak faith that is characteristic of the

American church. Speaking of the negative impact of secularism, Dallas Willard notes:

> The crushing weight of the secular outlook . . . permeates or pressures every thought we have today. Sometimes it even forces those who self-identify as Christian teachers to set aside Jesus' plain statements about the reality and total relevance of the kingdom of God and replace them with philosophical speculations whose only recommendation is their consistency with a 'modern' [i.e., contemporary] mind-set.
>
> The powerful though vague and unsubstantiated presumption is that something has been found out that renders a spiritual understanding of reality in the manner of Jesus simply foolish to those who are 'in the know.'"[6]

It is the subconscious fear that God is dead that is responsible for the loss of real, classic happiness among the American people. With genuine insight, Christopher Lasch correctly saw a connection between a secular perspective and a profound sense of despair and fatalism about life. To see why this connection is correct, suppose I invited you over to my house to play a game of Monopoly. When you arrive, I announce that the game is going to be a bit different. Before us is the Monopoly board, a set of jacks, a coin, the television remote, and a refrigerator in the corner of the room. I grant you the first turn, and puzzlingly, inform you that you may do anything you want: fill the board with hotels, throw the coin in the air, toss a few jacks, fix a sandwich, or turn on the television. You respond by putting hotels all over the board and smugly sit back as I take my turn. I respond by dumping the board upside down and tossing the coin in the air. Somewhat annoyed, you right the board and replenish it with hotels. I turn on the television and dump the board over again.

Now it wouldn't take too many cycles of this nonsense to recognize that it didn't really matter what you did with your turn, and here's why. There is no goal, no purpose to the "game" we are playing. Our successive turns form a series of one meaningless event after another. Why? Because if the game as a whole has no purpose, the individual moves within the game are pointless. Conversely, it is only in light of a game's actual purpose according to its inventor that the individual moves within the game take on significance. For example, if the purpose of Monopoly was to see who could lose their money first, all of a sudden, the utilities would be treasures, and Boardwalk and Park Place would become lethal properties!

Two points follow from this little thought experiment: (1) If we are playing "Monopoly," yet there is no purpose to the game, then it doesn't matter what we do with our turns. In fact, the very act of taking a turn becomes pointless and empty. (2) If the game has actually been invented by someone who established its goal or purpose, it is crucial that players know what that purpose is. Misinformation about the purpose can easily create a situation in which players actually harm themselves by exerting a dedicated effort to play the game if their efforts are directed at an end inconsistent with the game's actual goal. Sincerity is not enough.

This is where we stand today. There are pervasive, subtle, almost subconscious patterns of ideas in our culture that imply there is no meaning to life. All that is left is addiction to happiness, the instant satisfaction of desire, and a literal plague of deep anxiety that is affecting tens of millions of Americans. As it turns out, our beliefs are the rails on which our lives (including most of our anxiety) run. We almost always live up to—or down to—our actual beliefs. Our worldview—the set of things we actually believe about God, reality, meaning, value, what counts as success, what constitutes a good person and whether or not we are one, what we can and cannot know, and other significant topics—is the most important factor about our life. It's more important than having a flat stomach, being healthy, or fulfilling the American Dream.

In the climactic last chapter of *The Anxiety & Phobia Workbook*, psychologist and author Edmund J. Bourne zeroes in on the importance of meaning to life, spirituality, and God: "For some people, a lack of purpose and meaning in life can provide fertile ground for the development of panic attacks and phobias."[7] A page later, he observes that spirituality "refers not to any particular religion but to a basic sense of their being a larger purpose to life, as well as a larger power—a 'Higher Power,' if you will—that transcends the human order of things. *Not only may spirituality provide life with greater meaning, but it can help overcome anxiety directly because it leads to qualities such as inner peace, serenity, faith, and unconditional love.*"[8]

Apart from disagreeing with Bourne's vague, pluralistic theology, I believe he is onto something profound: While training oneself to have specific anxiety-defeating thoughts that are habitually triggered is good, a key theme of my recovery, it is also of great importance to develop a relationship with (the true!) God and derive meaning and purpose in life from a larger perspective. In fact, when trying to process and make sense of anxiety, it is important not to do so in light of our lives alone, in isolation from a bigger picture. Rather, such processing should be done in a broader context in which we first try to locate our life circumstances, our purpose for being here, and so on in light of God's greater mission for his people. And given our historical, family, and cultural context, as well as our gifts, talents, and responsibilities, we can locate our meaning and purpose in light of the role we each can play in God's larger and greater purposes. Developing a relationship with the biblical God, learning to trust and depend on him, and seeking to look beyond ourselves to serve others according to our specific circumstances and abilities are all extremely helpful in weakening anxiety's hold.

There's just one problem with all this. Sometimes God seems to be an uninterested, unavailable Being who seems to have forgotten his promises to be with and care for us. When we cry out to him in the midst of severe anxiety, he often seems to be a no-show. I am frequently asked what is my biggest problem with Christianity. To be honest, I am at a place in life where I no longer have doubts about the central truths of Christianity. Still, my biggest frustration with Christianity is that God simply seems to be a no-show at the very point when I most need him and when it would seem to be in his own interests to intervene. I have seen and heard eyewitness accounts of enough miracles to know without a doubt that they occur today. But I have also seen enough tragedies when I just don't get why God didn't seem to do anything about one of his children's suffering. His absence felt far too prevalent in both of my nervous breakdowns. I called and called on God, and seemingly nothing happened that was helpful—or so it seemed to me.

I am far from the only believer who has wrestled with this problem of a seemingly distant God. C. S. Lewis struggled profoundly with despair after the death of his wife, Joy, in 1960, after only three years of marriage. Here is one expression of his anguish and discouragement:

> Meanwhile, where is God? This is one of the most disquieting symptoms. When you are happy, so happy that you have no sense of needing Him, so happy that you are tempted to feel His claims upon you as an interruption, if you remember yourself and turn to Him with gratitude and praise, you will be—or so it feels—welcomed with open arms. But go to Him when your need is desperate, when all other help is vain, and what do you find? A door slammed in your face, and a sound of bolting and double bolting on the inside. After that, silence. You may as well turn away.[9]

There is no easy answer to the sense of abandonment by God that many of us have experienced, but I want to offer reflections that helped me with my anxiety in the face of this struggle by giving me a bigger and more biblical perspective on my suffering. I pray you will find them encouraging as well.

SUFFERING, SICKNESS, AND MIRACULOUS HEALING

The first thing we need to get clear about has to do with a distinction between suffering that is brought on by the bad actions of others, especially in connection with our witness for Christ, and sickness, including mental illnesses like anxiety and depression.[10] Though he allows sickness on a widespread scale, almost without exception, God does not want us to be sick and does not enjoy it when we are. Sickness is a result of the fall. Jesus greeted sickness as an enemy.

So while God allows sickness and we can, thankfully, grow from it, nevertheless, it is inherently evil, and we should do everything we can to get well. Jesus' attitude toward suffering versus sickness/demonization were very different. He told us to rejoice over suffering (Matthew 5:11–12; cf. Romans 5:3–4; James 1:2–5), but he never counseled someone to rejoice over being sick or to be patient because disease is helpful and redemptive (see Matthew 8:3; 12:16; Mark 1:41).

Suffering and sickness are different. We are called to suffer, but except in very rare cases, we are not called to be sick. You can almost always trust that God wants you well. Let me put this differently. In almost all cases, God wants us well and to be healed of our anxiety or depression. Thus, we should assume that God wants our anxiety or depression gone unless we have overwhelming reasons otherwise (e.g., they are essential to your calling). Here is a wise reminder from Francis MacNutt: "Too many Christians are broken in a destructive way—so badly broken that they cannot carry out the great commandment of loving God and neighbor. Their inner turmoil *prevents* them from carrying out God's will, and yet, paradoxically, they may still believe that such a sickness is God's will. Therefore, they feel no inclination to ask for release from what they believe God is imposing on them."[11]

In the first three centuries of Christianity, the church successfully and regularly offered healing for those who were sick. But as time went on, the church changed its views about sickness and the suffering it brings. Christian leaders in the fourth and fifth centuries proclaimed that the difference between the church and other religions or the unbelieving world was that the church alone regularly produces saints and spiritual heroes, virtuous people with Christlike character. And since suffering was an essential part of spiritual growth, suffering came to be seen as a blessing from God. To seek or pray for healing was considered wrong. As MacNutt puts it:

> This particular idea of sanctity [that suffering was a blessing essential to spiritual maturity] helped to destroy the common practice of praying for healing.
>
> For instance, if you were really serious about living as a committed Christian, you might regard your suffering and sickness as an opportunity to grow in

sanctity rather than as a curse—the wounding of your humanity—a curse that Jesus had come to conquer and overcome.

It turned the whole meaning of suffering and sickness upside down. Sickness came to be seen as a *blessing* permitted—if not actually sent—as a test by God in order to help you grow in holiness.[12]

In all likelihood, our anxiety and the suffering caused by it are, indeed, permitted by God, but it is not a blessing he wants us to receive and keep possessing. No, it is a curse due to the fallen world in which we live, and we should assume that God wants our anxiety gone. So we continue to pray for healing and ask others to lay hands on us and pray, even if God does not heal us.

In my experience, a very effective form of prayer for reducing anxiety and depression is what many call "soaking prayer." Since the term is used in so many ways, let me be clear how I am using it. Soaking prayer occurs when two or three people who are trained and experienced at this ask someone to lie down on a comfortable couch or recline in a relaxing recliner, and upon getting permission, lay hands on the person in appropriate places—e.g., the forehead, the shoulders, or the arms—and pray over them for anywhere from one to three hours. During that time, the person relaxes, closes their eyes, and receives the warmth, blessing, and love of God's presence and of those praying for them. If this sounds interesting to you, try calling solid churches in your area to find one that practices soaking prayer of this kind. You can always ask the church receptionist to describe exactly what happens in a session. Many have found it helpful to schedule two to four weeks in a row.

Additionally, while sickness and suffering are intrinsically evil, they can serve a greater good and can work with other circumstances in our lives to bring about good for those of us who love Jesus (Romans 8:28; Galatians 4:13–14). This means that even though anxiety is evil and, in general, not God's will for us, it still does not get to defeat us, because over time it will result in goodness that outweighs the suffering.

This is not a pie-in-the-sky statement. We all know believers who, time after time, give wonderful, heartfelt, gratitude-soaked testimonies to this truth. Usually, they say they would not want to go through the suffering again, but looking back, they see and are enjoying all the fruits that resulted from the suffering. Thus, at least we can have hope in the midst of anxiety that if we do undergo a longer period of suffering than we desire or think is fair, there will indeed be good that comes out of it.

Here are a few brief reflection points about suffering that may be worth pondering:[13]

- Suffering is an enemy of God. It is always intrinsically evil. But thank God, it can be instrumentally good: "You intended to harm me, but God intended it for good" (Genesis 50:20).
- We can give suffering meaning and purpose by providing it with a context. We can locate it in our and God's story.
- We need not waste our suffering. We can seek to let it form rather than deform us.

- In Christ, God himself has experienced suffering. He knows what we are going through; he gets it.
- Suffering humbles us, deepens our dependence on God, makes us value the good things in our lives, strengthens our relationship to God, and gives us a platform to help others.

Nevertheless, God still heals the sick, and we have the right to pray as many times as we want for healing (Luke 18:1–8). If we sense that the Holy Spirit has clearly indicated to us to stop praying for healing (and don't confuse weariness over not seeing results with the Holy Spirit telling you to stop!), then we can memorize 2 Corinthians 12:7–10 and practice adopting its approach. However, rather than God doing it all and healing us, his preferred way of acting is for us to be coworkers (1 Corinthians 3:9; 2 Corinthians 6:1; 3 John 8). We do our part; he does his. In this way, our actions count, but the result is more than can be explained by our efforts. We practice under his power and leadership the kind of things mentioned in this book, and we seek miraculous healing. Especially relevant is the need to find a church where people are trained in and practice the art of inner-healing ministry and prayer. This is most effective for mental illness, especially anxiety.

At this point, a question comes to mind: Why does God not answer prayers for healing? It's hard to know in a particular case, but the following reasons may help us maintain a hopeful perspective or do some helpful soul work:

1. LEGALISM AND LUKEWARM FAITH. These tend to push us away from God and to build barriers between us and him. They make it more difficult to come to God as to a tender Abba Papa and open up our heart cries to him. Self-examination here may be helpful, as long as we don't use it as an occasion to engage in negative self-talk that we are a loser, a bad person, and so forth. If we find something to confess, then we do it sincerely and rededicate ourselves to seeking and serving God with a whole heart.

2. UNBELIEF. Jesus did, in fact, heal some people in spite of their lack of faith. Still, the importance of faith (trust, confidence) of healing in the New Testament cannot be denied. So unbelief can be a hindrance to effective prayer—an unbelief that can be in the person or persons doing the praying or in the individual receiving prayer. We can't just will ourselves to have more faith at the moment than we do. If we try to crank up faith, we'll end up faking it. Instead, we simply do our best. Place whatever trust we currently have in God, and let things be what they are.

3. THE REDEMPTIVE VALUES OF SUFFERING. We've already discussed this, and it really is good news. While it is not our first line of defense in prayer for healing anxiety, it is good to know that we can grow in well-being in the midst of anxiety.

4. NOT REALLY WANTING TO GET WELL. Some people so identify with their anxiety and the desired

attention they receive from others because of it that they do not truly want to be healed, though this lack of desire is usually suppressed below conscious awareness. So if someone in this situation were asked if they want to be healed, they would most likely say "Yes!"— even though, deep down, they do not. This is called by psychologists "secondary gain." For example, if I'm sick, I may not want to get well because I enjoy the secondary gain of a lot of attention focused on me.

5. SICKNESS AS A RESULT OF SIN. Numerous studies have shown that leading a maturing Christian life has tremendous benefits for mental and physical health. Conversely, living a life of sin and not being willing to face it, to get help in putting it aside after it is earnestly confessed, or to even recognize its presence in one's life can contribute significantly to anxiety. So we can ask ourselves two questions: (1) Upon examining myself and seeking feedback from a close, safe friend, do I find a sin (or sins) in my life that have become habitual? (2) If so, is it really worth hanging on to that sin(s), especially in light of the health damage it is causing me in general and the anxiety it is producing in particular? Being omniscient and seeing the larger and longer picture, God knows that if he healed us now, greater harm would come to us over the long haul. This principle is self-explanatory, but it provides tremendous comfort when suffering from anxiety won't go away and God seems unwilling to provide help.

6. THE TIMING ISN'T RIGHT. This is an implication of point 5. Sometimes God knows that if he were to heal us now, it would hurt us in the long run. Given God's knowledge of the future, he may wait until a proper time so our suffering will be at work for maximum good in our lives.

7. DEMONIC INTERFERENCE WITH OUR PRAYERS. The Bible is clear that demons can hinder and delay our prayers getting to God (see Daniel 10, especially verses 10–14). If we suspect this may be the case, then we can (1) confess our sins and pray for cleansing (1 John 1:9), and (2) direct our prayers against the attacking demons, commanding them to leave us and our prayers alone by the authority of the name of Jesus Christ and because of his shed blood on the cross. Regarding demons, their influence on us, and our response to them, I highly recommend Charles Kraft's book *Defeating Dark Angels*, listed in the annotated bibliography in appendix 4.

Besides an earnest search for a reason that our prayers for healing aren't being answered, there is also the possibility of deep disappointment with God. Larry Crabb notes that God often seems like a fickle, random-acting Being. He asks, "How do we trust a fickle God who gives us a convenient place to park the day after we're told our loved one's tumor is malignant?"[14] Crabb goes on: "Is there anything we can hope for now, anything we can count on God to do for us in this life? . . . *How do we trust a sometimes disappointing, seemingly fickle God who fails to do for us what good friends, if they could, would do?"*[15]

Because we do not often talk with each other about our disappointment with God—that seems to be an evangelical taboo—we don't know what to do with it. And since this is such a common issue when one is suffering with anxiety, the double whammy can be enough to overwhelm any hope a person has for getting better. Since this topic is so important for anxiety sufferers, I will return to it later. But for now, here are a few brief points that have helped me to think about the problem.

1. I can express my anger to God honestly (Psalm 39; 88).
2. What can I honestly trust God for?
   - That in all things God works for my good, that no irredeemable harm will happen to me, and that I'll look back on my life and say it was worth it (Romans 8:28).
   - That I won't be exposed to trials or hardships I can't handle; if I can't handle it, God will provide a way out (1 Corinthians 10:13).
   - That heaven makes all this worthwhile (see John Burke, *Imagine Heaven*, listed in the annotated bibliography in the back of this book).
   - That God hears our prayers and occasionally answers them.
   - That I'm not alone. God is with me. Most of the time I don't sense that he's with me, but I still know he is aware of what's happening to me and loves me.
   - That the question to ask is this: To whom else can I go?

How to Handle and Express Our Disappointment with God

It is rightly said that God wants an honest, authentic, sincere relationship with us. Paul goes so far as to say that this is one of the major, if not *the* major, goals of his discipleship ministry and teaching: "The goal of this command is love, which comes from a *pure* heart and a *good* conscience and a *sincere* faith" (1 Timothy 1:5, emphasis mine). And the author of Hebrews reminds us that when we approach God, "let us draw near to God with a sincere heart" (Hebrews 10:22) This only makes sense because we can't fake God out. After all, "the Lord searches every heart and understands every desire and every thought" (1 Chronicles 28:9).

This means that if we are angry or disappointed with God, we should tell him. Such prayers from the Old Testament have come to be called "laments," which are passionate expressions of grief, sorrow, regret, or disappointment. To lament is to wail, moan, cry, or sob; to offer a complaint (a statement that a situation is unsatisfactory or unacceptable, often expressed in anger or confusion). Here is an example of a lament from the Old Testament prophet Habakkuk:

> How long, LORD, must I call for help,
>> but you do not listen?
> Or cry out to You, "Violence!"
>> but you do not save.
> Why do you make me look at injustice?

> Why do you tolerate wrongdoing?
> Destruction and violence are before me;
> > there is strife, and conflict abounds.
> Therefore the law is paralyzed,
> > and justice never prevails.
> The wicked hem in the righteous,
> > so that justice is perverted.
>
> *Habakkuk 1:2–4 (cf. Lamentations 3:1–18)*

Out of 150 psalms, 48 are individual laments, and 16 are corporate laments (for a total of 64). There are 15 psalms of trust, 20 of praise, and 13 of wisdom. Remember, the book of Psalms was the hymnbook for ancient Israel, and 43 percent of their congregational singing proved to be complaints and expressions of sadness and disappointment with God![16]

Why is this true? The Jewish worshipers wanted to approach God with sincere hearts, and they experienced a fundamental problem: God does not seem to keep his covenant (Psalm 44:17–26; cf. 89:34) or his promises (Psalm 9:9–10: "The LORD is a refuge for the oppressed, a stronghold in times of trouble. Those who know your name trust in you, for you, LORD, have never forsaken those who seek you"; see also Psalm 89). God saved in the past but seems not to in the present, so perhaps he is arbitrary, fickle, and unfair (see Psalm 44), or maybe he is absent, indifferent, aloof, and far away (see Psalm 10:1; 77:7–9). He does not always answer when we call out to him (see Psalm 22:3–6; 39:12; note that Psalms 39 and 88 are two of the saddest psalms in the Psalter because they end with no response from God, no hope, no resolution).

Many times God does not say how long the psalmist's suffering will last (see Psalm 13:1–4; 35:17). Sometimes the psalmist claims that God has become an enemy (see Psalm 88:8–9; cf. Lamentations 3:1–18, esp. verse 10: "like a bear lying in wait, like a lion in hiding"). These apparent features of God often become more of a struggle than our original source of pain. If we can't go to God and get help, we are in far deeper trouble than from our original suffering. Our problems raise crucial life-and-death questions: *Why should I trust God in the first place, and if I do, what does it actually mean to trust God? What can I expect from him? How can I claim his explicit promises that he himself seems to contradict and on which he has reneged?*

To get a feel for the various kinds of issues that provoked God's children to cry out to (or against!) him in lament, I urge you to take your time and read carefully the different psalms below. You may want to mark the ones that especially touch you, and if relevant, use them as beginning points for your own times of expressing lament to God.

TYPES OF LAMENT PRAYERS

A CRY OF PAIN (PSALM 80:4–7)

How long, LORD God Almighty,
    will your anger smolder
    against the prayers of your people?

You have fed them with the bread of tears;
>you have made them drink tears by the bowlful.
You have made us an object of derision to our neighbors,
>and our enemies mock us.
Restore us, God Almighty;
>make your face shine on us,
>that we may be saved.

A Cry of Anger (Psalm 44:11–13, 17–26)

You gave us up to be devoured like sheep
>and have scattered us among the nations.
You sold your people for a pittance,
>gaining nothing from their sale.
You have made us a reproach to our neighbors,
>the scorn and derision of those around us . . .
All this came upon us,
>though we had not forgotten you;
>we had not been false to your covenant.
Our hearts had not turned back;
>our feet had not strayed from your path.
But you crushed us and made us a haunt for jackals;
>you covered us over with deep darkness.
If we had forgotten the name of our God
>or spread out our hands to a foreign god,
would not God have discovered it,
>since he knows the secrets of the heart?
Yet for your sake we face death all day long;
>we are considered as sheep to be slaughtered.

Awake, Lord! Why do you sleep?

Rouse yourself! Do not reject us forever.

Why do you hide your face

and forget our misery and oppression?

We are brought down to the dust;

our bodies cling to the ground.

Rise up and help us.

A Cry of Confusion (Psalm 77:1–9)

I cried out to God for help;

I cried out to God to hear me.

When I was in distress, I sought the Lord;

at night I stretched out untiring hands,

and I would not be comforted.

I remembered you, God, and I groaned;

I meditated, and my spirit grew faint.

You kept my eyes from closing;

I was too troubled to speak.

I thought about the former days,

the years of long ago;

I remembered my songs in the night.

My heart meditated and my spirit asked:

Will the Lord reject forever?

Will he never show his favor again?

Has his unfailing love vanished forever?

Has his promise failed for all time?

Has God forgotten to be merciful?

Has he in anger withheld his compassion?"

A CRY OF COMPLAINT (PSALMS 6 AND 13)
Psalm 6

LORD, do not rebuke me in your anger
    or discipline me in your wrath.
Have mercy on me, LORD, for I am faint;
    heal me, LORD, for my bones are in agony.
My soul is in deep anguish.
    How long, LORD, how long?
Turn, LORD, and deliver me;
    save me because of your unfailing love.
Among the dead no one proclaims your name.
    Who praises you from the grave?
I am worn out from my groaning.
All night long I flood my bed with weeping
    and drench my couch with tears.
My eyes grow weak with sorrow;
    they fail because of all my foes.
Away from me, all you who do evil,
    for the LORD has heard my weeping.
The LORD has heard my cry for mercy;
    the LORD accepts my prayer.
All my enemies will be overwhelmed with shame and anguish;
    they will turn back and suddenly be put to shame.

Psalm 13

How long, LORD? Will you forget me forever?
    How long will you hide your face from me?
How long must I wrestle with my thoughts

' and day after day have sorrow in my heart?
　　How long will my enemy triumph over me?
Look on me and answer, LORD my God.
　　Give light to my eyes, or I will sleep in death,
and my enemy will say, "I have overcome him,"
　　and my foes will rejoice when I fall.
But I trust in your unfailing love;
　　my heart rejoices in your salvation.
I will sing the LORD's praise,
　　for he has been good to me.

A CRY OF ARGUMENT—SOMETIMES WITH AND SOMETIMES AGAINST GOD (PSALMS 22; 35; 39; 42; 43; 74; 88; 90; 102)

Look at the mocking tone of Psalm 74:11:

> Why do you [Lord] hold back your hand, your right hand?
> 　　Take it from the folds of your garment and destroy
> 　　[our enemy].

Psalm 90:13 (NASB) even enjoins God to repent:

> Do return, O LORD; how long will it be?
> And be sorry for [the NASB footnote reads, "Or *repent in regard to*] Your servants."

These psalms present what Old Testament scholars call a "*rîb*-pattern"—a legal-type brief consisting of a carefully thought-out, reasoned case against God.

This sort of prayer finds precedent in various places in the Old Testament. For example, before Jeremiah offers a reasoned argument in prayer to persuade God to act on his behalf, he begins, "You are always righteous, Lord, when I bring a case [*rîb*] before you" (Jeremiah 12:1). Elsewhere, Jeremiah does the same thing: "To you I have committed my cause [*rîb*]" (Jeremiah 20:12). Indeed, God actually invited his people to do this: "'Present your case [*rîb*],' says the Lord says. 'Set forth your arguments'" (Isaiah 41:21).

Terms related to *rîb* are *mishpat* ("I would state my case [*mishpat*] before him and fill my mouth with arguments" [Job 23:4]) and *yakakh* ("'Come now, and let us reason (*yakakh*—reason, argue, adjudicate) together,' says the Lord" [Isaiah 1:18 NASB]).

LAMENT'S THEOLOGICAL CONVICTIONS

We can feel the raw emotions dripping off each of these passages of lament. Now, obviously, when we are angry at God and express disappointment to him for appearing to fail us in one way or another, the hope is that a time will come when we realize that God is not the fickle culprit we thought he was. But the best way to get to that point is to be honest and start with where we really are, even if it's the place expressed in these psalms.

Expressing to God our honest feelings and beliefs is a good way to get things off our chest, stop stuffing our feelings, release anxiety, and begin a path toward a more intimate relationship with God. Clearly, the fact that God's people felt the freedom to express things to God like the ones we've just examined is based on foundational theological convictions. Here are some of them:

1. At the end of the day, God is indeed faithful, trustworthy, and caring, and he is a God who honors his promises (see Psalm 9:9–10).

2. God wants us to speak honestly with him and not pretend we're at a place that he knows we're really not at (see Jeremiah 12:1; 20:12).

3. God listens to and responds to reasonable points we make. He can be reasoned with (see Genesis 18:20–33; Isaiah 1:18).

4. God can and sometimes is willing to change (see Psalm 6:4–5; 80:14; 90:13; cf. Genesis 6:6; Jeremiah 18:7–10).

5. I'd add a few New Testament considerations: (1) Our question is Peter's question: "Lord, to whom shall we go?" (John 6:68). (2) God will not allow us to suffer more or longer than we can bear, so when we ask God "How much longer?" we are on solid ground. (3) God sees and has a bigger purpose than we do (see Acts 4:23–30).

6. Laments are the shadow side of faith. It is precisely because we take God seriously and desire to grow in faith and in our relationship with him that we engage in honest lament. If we were indifferent to God, we wouldn't waste our time with lament.

All these convictions raise some final questions: How can we deal with disappointment with God? If we seek to retain high faith expectations regarding God, won't that just make us vulnerable to further disappointment and disillusionment? If we lower our faith expectations, doesn't something die inside us? And is there a difference between hope and expectation? If so, what is that difference, and is it desirable to concentrate on retaining one and letting the other go when faced with disappointment with God?

Maintaining a biblically based worldview, a larger perspective on life as to its meaning and purpose, can place our struggle with anxiety or depression in a larger, hopeful perspective. And while God doesn't want us to be mentally ill, he often does not answer our prayers for relief and healing in the way we desire. Thus, it is important to learn how to express honestly and authentically our feelings and attitudes toward God in these times. There is biblical precedent for this, so we can go ahead and be honest.

I hope and pray that the things I have surveyed in this book, the tools that worked in such a life-giving way for me, will help you too as you journey through this sometimes painful and confusing life.

BULLET-POINT SUMMARY

- We are and feel largely what we think.
- The secular condition of contemporary life contributes to the current epidemic of anxiety and depression.
- Without God, there is no meaning, no purpose, to life, yet these are crucial for a proper, healing perspective on anxiety/depression.

- Our worldview is the most important aspect of our lives and our mental health.
- Knowing what to do when God seems distant, uninvolved, and a no-show when our need is great is critical for minimizing anxiety.
- God wants us to be well both physically and mentally.
- Suffering and sickness can have positive long-term benefits.
- There are several good reasons that God does not always answer prayers for healing.
- God wants an honest and authentic relationship with us. After all, he already knows how we feel and think about him before we tell him. So we *can* be honest.
- Learning and praying the lament psalms are good ways of handling our disappointments with God.
- We should remember the important theological assumptions that underlie the lament psalms.

Conclusion

PUTTING IT ALL
TOGETHER

Now that you have read this far, it would be natural to feel overwhelmed, especially if you are a fellow sufferer of anxiety and depression. I have suggested a large number of ideas and practices that helped me get rid of anxiety and depression. Where might you start in your own journey?

There is no one-size-fits-all answer to this question. The first thing I would tell anyone is to see a therapist and then a psychiatrist to see whether you might be helped by medications.

At the same time, you may want to peruse appendixes 1–4. In appendix 1, select a few verses—three to four would be fine—that you want to memorize and bring to mind in your time of contemplative prayer or at different times throughout your day. In appendix 2, you may find the two prayers of Dallas Willard to be soothing and hopeful. If so, you may want to copy them and place them on a mirror or on the refrigerator so you see and reflect on them frequently. In appendix 4,

I've provided an annotated bibliography of books I've read and found helpful. I believe it is a good idea to continue reading about mental health—as long as it doesn't make us feel pressured. If it does, then we should set the reading aside and perhaps in a few months start reading again. If you choose to read any of the suggested books, I recommend especially beginning with one of the five books listed at the start of the bibliography.

Finally, let me say an important word about appendix 3. You will see that it contains all the summary bullet points from the book. I'd encourage you to get a cup of coffee or tea, turn to the appendix, and take your time mulling over it.

Some of the bullet points provide *general reminders* or things to keep in mind that can help reorient our approach to life in ways that reduce stress, anxiety, or depression. For example, we are not alone or messed up because of our problems; rather, we are simply broken like everyone else. Or we have a moral duty to be happy, so working on our anxiety or depression is not a luxury; it is a moral imperative—a fact that should motivate us to stick with it. You get the idea. You may want to check off five to ten of the ideas you find most helpful, turn them into a list, and place them somewhere in your home or at work where they can remind you of them.

Some bullet points describe specific habit-forming practices—for example, the HeartMath exercises of Quick Coherence and the Heart Lock-In Technique or contemplative prayer. With the support of your therapist, you may want to try some of these practices yourself. The most important point I learned is this: anxiety and depression are significantly formed habits residing in the brain and body (especially the heart muscle and nervous system), and these habits can be largely replaced with peaceful and joyful habits by regularly engaging in the right repetitive habit-forming exercises.

When I first started these practices as I awoke in the morning and began my routines such as taking a shower, making coffee, and so on, I would do two things: (1) select four or five things I appreciated (one was the joy I anticipated in drinking my morning coffee) and express them to God as a form of gratitude; and (2) pray Psalm 139:23–24: "Search me, God, and know my heart; test me and know my anxious thoughts. See if there is any offensive way in me, and lead me in the way everlasting [the way of shalom and flourishing]."

Next, I would find a quiet, private, and comfortable place and have ten minutes of contemplative prayer. When I began this practice, I spent about a minute searching my body for any uncomfortable signs of tension or anxiety, placed my hand on that area, and spoke God's peace, relaxation, safety, and healing to that location. My area is usually my head, so I often started (and still do this daily, two and a half years later!) my prayer time by placing my hands on my head, picturing the Lord Jesus placing his hands on top of mine, and speaking peace and healing to my head. This lasted for about one minute.

Then I placed my hand over my heart muscle, and for two minutes, I performed the HeartMath Quick Coherence exercise. Then I prayed four Bible passages that are very special to me (1 Peter 5:6–7; Proverbs 3:5–6; Isaiah 26:3; and Psalm 46:10). This took a few minutes. When I prayed 1 Peter

5:6–7, it allowed me to let go of control of my life ("humble yourselves, therefore, under God's mighty hand"), and then I cast "all [my] anxiety on him." I did not go over each one individually. That would distract me from the purpose of contemplative prayer (to attach to or connect intimately with God) and would take too long. I just placed all my anxiety in God's hand as one big bundle. Then I always finished with Psalm 46:10 because it is the perfect entrance to the rest of my time.

As I silently prayed Psalm 46:10, I simply sat quietly while opening my heart to God and being receptive to whatever way he wanted to connect with me or speak to me. If nothing happened, I still ended the time with a peaceful, quieted mind and heart. Early on, my mind wandered more than it does now, so I would simply bring my focus back on God by offering to him a word or phrase of prayer, such as "Abba," "Papa," "Jesus," "peace," "I receive you," "I love you dearly," or something like that. I showed self-compassion as I learned to do this because it can be frustrating in the early stages before it becomes a habit.

Throughout each day, I sought to practice four things as many times as I could or as a need arose: (1) Schwartz's Four-Step Solution (especially using it to train myself to live in the day and not in the future), (2) the HeartMath Quick Coherence exercise, (3) brainstorming practical ways to get rid of as much stress in my life as possible, and (4) offering expressions of gratitude to God.

In the evening as I reflected on my day (or at times during the day when I felt it necessary), I would express my disappointment with God if the day was hard and my anxiety or depression did not seem to be getting better. Often I used a lament psalm to help me. I would only do this if it was really needed and was the best way I could express myself to God honestly and authentically.

My time in bed before drifting off to sleep was crucial. At the beginning of learning these practices, I would go to bed twenty to thirty minutes early and engage in contemplative prayer, just like I had done in the morning. But there was one difference. During the entire time of prayer, I lay on my back and replaced the HeartMath Quick Coherence exercise with the Heart Lock-In Technique. All this means is that I would stay with my heart muscle for ten to fifteen minutes instead of for one to two minutes. My goal was that this period of contemplative prayer would put me in a mood of peace and safety and would place me in God's presence experientially. This did two things for me: it helped me go to sleep more quickly, and it placed God and my connection with him in my heart and mind as I fell asleep.

After three or four months, all these things became habits that I still perform daily without thinking about them. They actually become second nature. In general, it takes a little more than two months to really form a new habit, and I suggest it takes from two to five months to make these practices second nature. I experienced a lot of stops and starts along the way. Fortunately, I didn't have to wait for five months to experience the anxiety/depression-reducing effects. These began very quickly, since the practices are themselves intrinsically healthy in a psychological, spiritual, and physical way.

If you adopt these practices or others suggested by your therapist, just like a jogger who misses a day or two of running, you may find you miss them when skipped. They can become exercises you really look forward to. For me, such practices, along with medication and therapy, brought tremendous benefits in my struggle with anxiety and depression. Wherever you may be in your journey through anxiety and depression, my heartfelt desire in writing this book is that you may find similar benefits for yourself.

Appendix 1

ENCOURAGING VERSES

"Peace I leave with you; my peace I give you. I do not give to you as the world gives. Do not let your hearts be troubled and do not be afraid."

John 14:27

Search me, God, and know my heart;
    test me and know my anxious thoughts.
See if there is any offensive way in me,
    and lead me in the way everlasting [the way of
        shalom and flourishing].

Psalm 139:23–24

"Be still [let go and relax], and know [by experience] that I am God."

Psalm 46:10

Thou wilt keep him in perfect peace, whose mind is stayed on thee: because he trusteth in thee.

Isaiah 26:3 KJV

My heart is not proud, LORD,
>   my eyes are not haughty;
I do not concern myself with great matters
>   or things too wonderful for me.
But I have calmed and quieted myself;
>   I am like a weaned child with its mother;
>   like a weaned child I am content.
Israel, put your hope in the LORD
>   both now and forevermore.

Psalm 131

"So do not fear, for I am with you;
>   do not be dismayed, for I am your God.
I will strengthen you and help you;
>   I will uphold you with my righteous right hand."

Isaiah 41:10

"Do not be afraid; do not be discouraged, for the LORD
your God will be with you wherever you go."

Joshua 1:9

Trust in the LORD with all your heart
>   and lean not on your own understanding;
in all your ways submit to him,
>   and he will make your paths straight.

Proverbs 3:5–6

Trust in the LORD and do good;

    dwell in the land and enjoy safe pasture.

Take delight in the LORD,

    and he will give you the desires of your heart.

Commit your way to the LORD;

    trust in him and he will do this.

Psalm 37:3–5

Commit to the LORD whatever you do,

    and he will establish your plans.

The LORD works out everything to its proper end.

Proverbs 16:3–4

"Please don't put us through trials,

    but deliver us from everything bad."

Matthew 6:13 (Dallas Willard paraphrase)

No test or trial has overtaken you but such as is common to man; and God is faithful, who will not allow you to be tested beyond what you are able, but with the trial will provide the way of escape also, so that you will be able to endure it.

1 Corinthians 10:13 NASB,
with my exegetical correction

"Therefore do not worry about tomorrow, for tomorrow will worry about itself. Each day has enough trouble of its own."

Matthew 6:34

"Do not let your hearts be troubled. You believe in God; believe also in me."

John 14:1

Do not be anxious about anything, but in every situation, by prayer and petition, with thanksgiving, present your requests to God. And the peace of God, which transcends all understanding, will guard your hearts and your minds in Christ Jesus.

Philippians 4:6–7

Humble yourselves, therefore, under God's mighty hand, that he may lift you up in due time. Cast all your anxiety on him because he cares for you.

1 Peter 5:6–7

"The LORD bless you
and keep you;
the LORD make his face shine on you
and be gracious to you;
the LORD turn his face toward you
and give you peace."

Numbers 6:24–26

Appendix 2

SOOTHING, ENCOURAGING, UPLIFTING QUOTES FROM DALLAS WILLARD

DALLAS WILLARD'S PARAPHRASE OF THE LORD'S PRAYER

> Dear Father always near us,
> may your name be treasured and loved,
> may your rule be completed in us—
> may your will be done here on earth
> in just the way it is done in heaven.
> Give us today the things we need today,
> and forgive us our sins and impositions on you
> as we are forgiving all who in any way offend us.
> Please don't put us through trials,
> but deliver us from everything bad.
> Because you are the one in charge,
> and you have all the power,

and the glory too is all yours—forever—
which is just the way we want it!

From A Divine Conspiracy (San Francisco:
HarperSanFrancisco, 1998), 269

A Prayer of Dallas Willard

My prayer for you—

That you would have a rich life of joy and power, abundant in supernatural results, with a constant, clear vision of never-ending life in God's World before you, and of the everlasting significance of your work day by day.

A radiant life and death.

From the bookmark shared with folks
who attended the memorial services

Appendix 3

BULLET-POINT SUMMARIES OF EVERY CHAPTER

This checklist is meant to provide a quick way to access the main points of the book. It may be useful to glance over it from time to time in order to be reminded of a point that was meaningful to you. For details about each bullet point, you can consult the relevant pages where it was discussed.

CHAPTER 1

- Extrabiblical knowledge is helpful for defeating anxiety and depression.
- The Bible's holistic, functional view of humanity implies that we should launch our attack against anxiety and depression by using tools that address all aspects of ourselves (e.g., medication to address the brain, psychology to address the mind or emotions, and biblical, spiritual practices to address the spirit).

- One of your faculties (e.g., the faculty of emotion) can impact positively or negatively other faculties (e.g., the faculty of desire, choice, mind).
- Anxiety and depression are related to what is happening in the brain, and medications may be of real help in treating them.
- Anxiety and depression are significantly formed habits residing in the brain and body, and they can be largely replaced with peaceful and joyful habits by regularly engaging in the right repetitive habit-forming exercises.

CHAPTER 2

- If you have anxiety, you are not alone, weird, a spiritual failure, or hopeless.
- Stress, stress, stress is a major cause of anxiety. Get rid of it!
- There is reasonable hope that you can defeat anxiety.
- Among the several causes of anxiety, select the ones with which you most identify.
- Anxiety is a surface feeling that often hides deeper feelings—embarrassment, fear, grief, helplessness, hurt, loneliness, sadness. With which do you most identify?
- Don't waste your suffering.
- You have a moral duty to be happy.
- By adopting a certain approach to life, one that includes the proper regimen of habit-forming practices, you can defeat anxiety and become much happier.

- Self-compassion is an appropriate, biblically based feeling and attitude to take toward yourself. There are certain exercises that enhance self-compassion.
- Cultivate the habit of making intentional free choices that produce peace and well-being.

CHAPTER 3

- Anxiety is largely a habit wired or grooved into the brain and nervous system.
- Replacing old thinking habits with new thinking habits through certain daily practices helps to get rid of anxiety.
- How we think largely affects how we feel.
- Our self-talk goes largely unnoticed, and with the aid of the Holy Spirit, we must learn to notice it more regularly.
- The Four-Step Solution can be practiced several times a day: relabel, reframe, refocus, revalue.
- We need to identify our most frequently used distorted thinking traps.
- Focusing requires getting into a flow.
- We should avoid ruminating about negative self-talk.
- The HeartMath Solution can deal effectively with obsessive thoughts one cannot get out of one's mind by direct effort.
- We don't need to battle obsessive thoughts in our mind. Instead, we can disempower them in our heart region.

CHAPTER 4

- Anxiety affects physical health.

- Daily habit-forming practices can replace anxiety brain or body grooves and habits with peace and joy body or brain grooves and habits.
- Daily engagement in contemplative prayer for at least twelve minutes can change brain structure.
- You can learn and practice your own adaptation of the five steps of contemplative prayer listed in this chapter.
- Negative criticisms of contemplative prayer fail to be convincing.
- Of all personality traits, gratitude has one of the strongest links to mental health and satisfaction.
- How we label things makes a big difference in our emotional lives.
- The habit of expressing gratitude turns one from seeing a glass half empty to seeing it half full.
- We can all express gratitude a few times daily for a handful of things we are really grateful for, including the "little" things.
- Four important aspects of gratitude are intensity, frequency, span, and density.
- Some find it helpful to write daily in a gratitude journal.
- I encourage you to write and deliver a gratitude letter once a month.

CHAPTER 5

- See a primary care physician or a psychiatrist for advice on antianxiety/antidepressant medications suitable for your specific situation.

- Antianxiety/antidepressant medications are so good today that few people need to suffer from severe anxiety or depression. But they don't work for everyone, and they can have side effects.
- Taking medications for negative psychological feelings or moods is biblically based.
- Antianxiety/antidepressant medications can be fruitfully depicted as vitamins for the brain that supply what the brain is currently not able to provide for itself.
- In general, and for many people, prescription medications for anxiety and depression are more effective than "natural" remedies.
- Medications lower the intensity of anxiety/depression so spiritual/psychological practices can be utilized more effectively.
- In my experience, it's best not to address anxiety/depression with medications alone, but to be holistic and also use spiritual and psychological tools.
- EMDR therapy can be an effective supplement to talk therapy for releasing the power of isolated and deeply lodged painful feelings and memories. What has worked well for me is tapping in (1) a safe, peaceful place; (2) images of nurturing figures; (3) images of protectors; (4) figures who provide inner wisdom. Qualities necessary for better coping, such as courage, can also be tapped in.
- The HeartMath exercises of Quick Coherence and the Heart Lock-In Technique are most effective if practiced regularly.

CHAPTER 6

- We are and feel largely what we think.
- The secular condition of contemporary life contributes to the current epidemic of anxiety and depression.
- Without God, there is no meaning, no purpose, to life, yet these are crucial for a proper, healing perspective on anxiety/depression.
- Our worldview is the most important aspect of our lives and our mental health.
- Knowing what to do when God seems distant, uninvolved, and a no-show when our need is great is critical for minimizing anxiety.
- God wants us to be well both physically and mentally.
- Suffering and sickness can have positive long-term benefits.
- There are several good reasons that God does not always answer prayers for healing.
- God wants an honest and authentic relationship with us. After all, he already knows how we feel and think about him before we tell him. So we *can* be honest.
- Learning and praying the lament psalms are good ways of handling our disappointments with God.
- We should remember the important theological assumptions that underlie the lament psalms.

Appendix 4

ANNOTATED BIBLIOGRAPHY OF TOOLS FOR ANXIETY, DEPRESSION, AND SPIRITUAL/ PSYCHOLOGICAL HEALTH

Note: starred books are highly recommended; the more stars, the more highly recommended.

MY FIRST CHOICES THAT ARE MUST-READS
Note: These are in order of preference.

**Lyubomirsky, Sonia. *The How of Happiness: A Scientific Approach to Getting the Life You Want.* New York: Penguin, 2007.

> The best book on happiness available. It contains twelve happiness strategies, along with a self-test to help determine which strategy is the most important one to employ.

**Elliott, Charles, and Laura Smith. *Overcoming Anxiety for Dummies*. 2nd ed. Hoboken, NJ: Wiley, 2010.

**Smith, Laura, and Charles Elliott. *Depression for Dummies*. Hoboken, NJ: Wiley, 2003.

> These books are very easy to read and cover the waterfront of ideas and supports for dealing with anxiety and depression.

**Schwartz, Jeffrey, and Rebecca Gladding. *You Are Not Your Brain: The 4-Step Solution for Changing Bad Habits, Ending Unhealthy Thinking, and Taking Control of Your Life*. New York: Penguin, 2011.

> The best book on learning how to spot and get rid of false, destructive self-talk by using the authors' four-step method.

**Childre, Doc, and Deborah Rozman. *Transforming Stress: The HeartMath Solution for Relieving Worry, Fatigue, and Tension*. Oakland, CA: New Harbinger, 2005.

> An incredibly helpful book for eliminating stress, anxiety, and depression by using a few simple techniques that involve connecting to what is in your heart muscle and heart area.

**Amen, Daniel, and Lisa Routh. *Healing Anxiety and Depression*. New York: Putnam, 2003.

> This book has a self-test to help you determine which of the seven different kinds of anxiety and depression you have. It contains a lot of strategies for improvement, including helpful information on natural remedies.

A Christian View of the Soul

Goetz, Stewart, and Charles Taliaferro. *A Brief History of the Soul*. Malden, MA: Wiley-Blackwell, 2011.

> A delightful presentation of the history of how the soul has been conceived from Plato to the present.

Moreland, J. P. *The Soul: How We Know It's Real and Why It Matters*. Chicago: Moody, 2014.

> Contains a definition of consciousness and the soul, along with a defense of the claim that these are immaterial and not physical.

*Cooper, John. *Body, Soul, and Life Everlasting: Biblical Anthropology and the Monism-Dualism Debate*. Rev. ed. Grand Rapids: Eerdmans, 2000.

> The best biblical defense of the soul in print. Cooper examines carefully a number of Old Testament and New Testament passages. A rich scriptural study.

Information about Prescription Medication/Psychiatric Drugs

*Albers, Lawrence, Rhoda Hahn, and Christopher Reist. *Handbook of Psychiatric Drugs*. 2011 ed. Blue Jay, CA: Current Clinical Strategies, 2010.

> An absolutely first-rate tool. A mere 117 pages, it lists virtually all the drugs psychiatrists use, along with important information about them.

Gorman, Jack. *The Essential Guide to Psychiatric Drugs*. 4th. ed. New York: St. Martin's, 2007.

> Discusses what psychiatric drugs are, how they work,

and which ones address which disorders, side effects, and so forth.

PSYCHOLOGICAL WORKS FOR TREATING ANXIETY/DEPRESSION

Amen, Daniel. *Magnificent Mind at Any Age: Natural Ways to Unleash Your Brain's Maximum Potential*. New York: Three Rivers, 2008.

> Describes a whole host of natural ways to cultivate and maintain a healthy brain.

Beattie, Melody. *The New Codependency: Help and Guidance for Today's Generation*. New York: Simon & Schuster, 2009.

> Beattie is the expert on codependency, and this is her latest offering on the subject. This is pretty much everything you wanted to know about codependency but were afraid to ask!

*Bourne, Edmund. *The Anxiety & Phobia Workbook*. 5th ed. Oakland, CA: New Harbinger, 2010.

> This is the gold standard used by therapists and psychiatrists. Coming in at 481 pages, it goes into detail about virtually all the issues surrounding anxiety and phobias. It is written at an accessible level to an ordinary reader.

*Bourne, Edmund, and Lorna Garano. *Coping with Anxiety: 10 Simple Ways to Relieve Anxiety, Fear, and Worry*. 2nd ed. Oakland, CA.: New Harbinger, 2016.

> This is a really good book. It is chock-full of helpful ideas about handling anxiety. In particular, it covers ten different coping strategies in a brief yet helpful way.

*Emmons, Robert. *Thanks! How Practicing Gratitude Can Make You Happier*. Boston: Houghton Mifflin, 2007.
> Emmons's book is a study of the importance of gratitude and a presentation of different ways of expressing gratitude.

———. *Gratitude Works! A 21-Day Program for Creating Emotional Prosperity*. San Francisco: Jossey-Bass, 2013.
> Presents specific suggestions for expressing gratitude in different ways, along with a twenty-one-day program for creating emotional prosperity.

*Greenberger, Dennis, and Christine Padesky. *Mind over Mood: Change How You Feel by Changing the Way You Think*. 2nd ed. New York: Guilford, 2016.
> An informative workbook for learning how to use cognitive behavioral therapy to spot, disempower, and replace negative self-talk.

Hart, Archibald. *The Anxiety Cure: You Can Find Emotional Tranquillity and Wholeness*. Nashville: Nelson, 1999.
> Written by the former dean of the Fuller School of Psychology, this book takes a multipronged approach to dealing with anxiety, with an emphasis placed on medications and cognitive behavioral therapy.

Leaf, Caroline. *Who Switched Off My Brain? Controlling Toxic Thoughts and Emotions*. Rev. ed. Southlake, TX: Thomas Nelson, 2009.
> Leaf describes how toxic thoughts are rooted in and affect the brain, but due to neuroplasticity, we can change our brains. She provides a strategy for doing this with respect to twelve toxic thoughts.

Luciani, Joseph. *Self-Coaching: The Powerful Program to Beat Anxiety and Depression.* 2nd ed. Hoboken, NJ: Wiley, 2007.

> This book is a very hopeful, commonsense approach to helping yourself get over anxiety.

Lyons, Rebekah. *Freefall to Fly: A Breathtaking Journey toward a Life of Meaning.* Carol Stream, IL: Tyndale, 2013.

> A personal story of a highly successful, driven woman who, after a nervous breakdown, learned to journey toward a life of meaning and to set aside anxiety and depression along the way.

Weekes, Claire. *Self-Help for Your Nerves: Learn to Relax and Enjoy Life Again by Overcoming Stress and Fear.* Rev. ed. London: Thorsons, 2015.

> While Weekes presents a number of aids for getting rid of anxiety, the real value of the book lies in her incredibly accurate description of one who is suffering from acute anxiety. If others don't understand what you are going through, have them read this book.

*Whitfield, Charles. *Healing the Child Within: Discovery and Recovery for Adult Children of Dysfunctional Families.* Deerfield Beach, FL: Health Communications, 1987.

> This is the classic book on identifying, finding, and healing the child within us and for spotting and getting rid of codependency.

Wilder, E. James, Edward Khouri, Chris Coursey, and Shelia Sutton. *Joy Starts Here: The Transformation Zone.* East Peoria, IL: Shepherd's House, 2013.

A book that defines joy as relationship and goes on to describe how to set aside dysfunctional relationships in favor of healthy ones, all with a view to forming joyful communities.

Works That Focus on the Brain and the Body

Childre, Doc, and Howard Martin. *The HeartMath Solution.* San Francisco: HarperSanFrancisco, 1999.

This is the book that covers the discovery of the HeartMath technique and goes into depth as to how to practice it. This book demonstrates that the HeartMath practice is not a New Age technique, but is a medical practice recommended by doctors.

*Gendlin, Eugene. *Focusing.* Rev. ed. New York: Bantam, 1981.

Gendlin was the first to discover mindfulness and focusing as a tool for body scanning. The book presents a picture of what focusing is and is not, along with some practical steps to take in learning how to focus.

Grand, David. *Brainspotting: The Revolutionary New Therapy for Rapid and Effecive Change.* Boulder, CO: Sounds True, 2013.

One of the most recent therapies for anxiety, brainspotting goes directly to the brain. Grand does a good job of describing the technique and offering ways to practice it.

Henslin, Earl. *This Is Your Brain on Joy: A Revolutionary Program for Balancing Mood, Restoring Brain Health, and Nurturing Spiritual Growth.* Nashville: Nelson, 2008.

Henslin does a pretty thorough job of describing the different regions of the brain and how they are related to anxiety, depression, and so on. He offers ways to take care of those parts of the brain so as to release more joy in one's life.

Moll, Rob. *What Your Body Knows About God: How We Are Designed to Connect, Serve, and Thrive.* Downers Grove, IL: InterVarsity, 2014.

Moll explains the role of the brain in spiritual transformation, along with a description of how spiritual practices transform the brain and nervous system. He concludes that our bodies were made for God and function best when we seek him fully.

Levine, Peter. *Healing Trauma: A Pioneering Program for Restoring the Wisdom of Your Body.* Boulder, CO: Sounds True, 2008.

Levine focuses on the way trauma is stored in the body and how focusing can help release it.

*Parnell, Laurel. *Tapping In: A Step-by-Step Guide to Activating Your Healing Resources through Bilateral Stimulation.* Boulder, CO: Sounds True, 2008.

This is an excellent self-help book that shows the reader how to use EMDR and bilateral stimulation on himself or herself in various types of ways.

A Brief List of Spiritual Formation Books of Help to Me

Note: I had to leave out many worthy books.

*Foster, Richard. *Celebration of Discipline: The Path to Spiritual Growth.* 40th anniv. ed. New York: HarperCollins, 2018.

> This is, in my view, the classic work on spiritual
> disciplines and how to practice them.

Hagberg, Janet and Robert Guelich. *The Critical Journey: Stages in the Life of Faith*. 2nd ed. Salem, WI: Sheffield, 2005.

> This is a good book that traces the stages of spiritual
> development; describes their characteristics, pitfalls,
> and strengths; and talks about issues in transitioning
> into the next phase.

*Keating, Thomas. *Open Mind, Open Heart*. 20th anniv. ed. New York: Continuum, 2006.

> A classic book on centering or contemplative prayer
> (though Keating does distinguish between the two).
> It will help you understand the purpose, practice, and
> pitfalls of this discipline.

Kehoe, Richard. *Transforming Love: A Journey in Spiritual Formation*. Highland, CA: Journey into Light, 2014.

> An easy-to-read book with short chapters and engaging
> questions after each chapter. A great book for a small
> group.

Moreland, J.P. and Klaus Issler. *The Lost Virtue of Happiness: Discovering the Disciplines of the Good Life*. Colorado Springs: NavPress, 2006.

> A book that carefully distinguishes contemporary from
> classical/biblical notions of happiness and describes
> some ways to become happier in the biblical sense.

*Moreland, J. P. *Kingdom Triangle: Recover the Christian Mind, Renovate the Soul, Restore the Spirit's Power*. Grand Rapids: Zondervan, 2007.

The book sets the spiritual life against the backdrop of two influential worldviews that distort spirituality. It goes on to suggest that three things must be kept in balance for a healthy Christian life: the development of a Christian mind, the cultivation of character and a tender heart, and the experience of kingdom/Holy Spirit power.

van Kaam, Adrian. *Spirituality and the Gentle Life*. Denville, NJ: Dimension, 1974.

A deep spiritual and psychological treatment of what a gentle approach to life looks like, how to develop it, and how to deal with hinderances.

*Willard, Dallas. *Hearing God: Developing a Conversational Relationship with God*. 3rd ed. Downers Grove, IL: InterVarsity, 1999.

A sane, biblical, and experiential treatment of how to cultivate the ability to hear God speak to you.

*————. *Renovation of the Heart: Putting on the Character of Christ*. Colorado Springs: NavPress, 2002.

A thoughtful treatment of the various aspects of the human person (the mind, emotions, will, body, social self, soul) and how to bring them into conformity with the kingdom of God.

*————. *Knowing Christ Today: Why We Can Trust Spiritual Knowledge*. San Francisco: HarperOne, 2009.

A development of the importance of taking Christian teaching as a source of knowledge of reality and not something to be accepted by blind faith.

*———. *Life Without Lack: Living in the Fullness of Psalm 23.*
Nashville: Nelson: 2018.

> A deep, calming, healing presentation of Psalm 23 in all
> its richness, focusing on how the reader can move closer
> to living a contented life without worry or fear.

BIBLICAL PERSPECTIVES ON SUFFERING AND DISAPPOINTMENT WITH GOD

Crabb, Larry. *Shattered Dreams: God's Unexpected Path to Joy.*
Colorado Springs: WaterBrook, 2001.

> This is a hard-hitting book in which Crabb lays out the
> fact that God seems to be a disappointment so much
> of the time. However, he offers reasons why we are
> mistakenly disappointed with God and provides help
> for avoiding disillusionment with God.

Yancey, Philip. *Disappointment with God: Three Questions
No One Asks Aloud.* 25th anniv. ed. Grand Rapids:
Zondervan, 2015.

> Yancey addresses three questions: (1) Is God unfair?
> (2) Is God silent? (3) Is God hidden? He works on
> these questions in the context of all of our journeys
> when God seems to be absent when we need
> him most.

*———. *Where Is God When It Hurts?* Grand Rapids:
Zondervan, 1990.

> Yancey addresses the questions of why there are such
> things as pain and suffering, along with discussing how
> we respond to and cope with pain and suffering.

HELPFUL WORKS ON HEALING PRAYER AND WHY GOD DOES NOT ALWAYS ANSWER

*MacNutt, Francis. *Healing.* Rev. ed. Notre Dame, IN: Ave Maria, 1999.

> This is the key book on the ins and outs of healing prayer. Excellent.

———. *The Power to Heal.* Notre Dame, IN: Ave Maria, 1977.

> This is a further elaboration on his earlier book, *Healing,* which first came out in 1974.

Deere, Jack. *Surprised by the Power of the Spirit: Discovering How God Speaks and Heals Today.* Grand Rapids: 1993.

> This is a comprehensive biblical defense of a Vineyard approach to healing. It also contains a lot of practical advice about healing prayer.

HELPFUL WORKS ON THE DEMONIC

*Kraft, Charles. *Defeating Dark Angels: Breaking Demonic Oppression in the Believer's Life.* 3rd ed. Grand Rapids: Chosen, 2016.

> In my opinion, this the best book for understanding the demonic and for learning how to deal with demons.

*MacNutt, Francis. *Deliverance from Evil Spirits: A Practical Manual.* 2nd. ed. Grand Rapids: Chosen, 2009.

> This is a very close second to Kraft's book. It is also very helpful and balanced in this area.

Many people have fears and anxiety resulting from doubts that God exists, that Jesus actually rose from the dead, that there is really such a thing as life after death, or that God still answers prayers, heals the sick, and does miraculous things for his children.

The next six sections provide resources to help you with these worrisome doubts. After a section on God's existence and one on the resurrection of Jesus, there are three sections on evidence for life after death, followed by a closing section recounting credible stories of God's miraculous care in our own time.

EVIDENCE FOR THE EXISTENCE OF GOD

Note: These are accessible works that give evidence for God's existence and consider arguments against God's existence.

Moreland, J. P. *The God Question: An Invitation to a Life of Meaning.* Eugene, OR: Harvest House, 2009.

*Moreland, J. P., and Tim Muehlhoff. *The God Conversation: Using Stories and Illustrations to Explain Your Faith.* Downers Grove, IL: InterVarsity, 2007.

> *The God Conversation* is easier to read and a bit less technical than *The God Question.*

EVIDENCE FOR THE RESURRECTION OF JESUS

*Craig, William Lane. *The Son Rises: The Historical Evidence for the Resurrection of Jesus.* 2nd. ed. Eugene, OR: Wipf & Stock, 2000.

*McDowell, Josh, and Sean McDowell. *More Than a Carpenter: His Story Might Change Yours.* Rev. ed. Carol Stream, IL: Tyndale, 2009.

Strobel, Lee. *The Case for Christ: A Journalist's Personal Investigation of the Evidence for Jesus*. Rev. ed. Grand Rapids: Zondervan, 2016.

Wallace, J. Warner. *Cold-Case Christianity: A Homicide Detective Investigates the Claims of the Gospel*. Colorado Springs: Cook, 2013.

> An absolutely fascinating, easy-to-read book. Wallace, a homicide detective who has appeared on shows such as *Dateline*, *FOX News*, and *Court TV*, applies his detective craft to the claims of the Gospels and concludes there is overwhelming evidence for their historical reliability.

BOOKS MAKING THE CASE FOR THE REALITY OF NEAR-DEATH EXPERIENCES

Note: These books contain wonderful stories of near-death experiences, but their strength is that they give the evidence for why we should trust these accounts and respond to all the objections that skeptics raise against NDEs. Very persuasive books. In my opinion, Burke is the best, followed by Miller and then Long.

Atwater, P. M. H., and David H. Morgan. *The Complete Idiot's Guide to Near-Death Experiences*. Indianapolis, IN: Alpha, 2000.

**Burke, John. *Imagine Heaven: Near-Death Experiences, God's Promises, and the Exhilarating Future That Awaits You*. Grand Rapids: Baker, 2015.

*Long, Jeffrey. *Evidence of the Afterlife: The Science of Near-Death Experiences.* San Francisco: HarperOne, 2010.

*Miller, J. Steve. *Near-Death Experiences as Evidence for the Existence of God and Heaven: A Brief Introduction in Plain Language.* Acworth, GA: Wisdom Creek, 2012.

COMPENDIA OF NDES

Note: These books contain a different near-death experience story in each chapter, with the result that many brief and inspiring stories are in these books.

*Bell, James Stewart, comp. *Angels, Miracles, and Heavenly Encounters: Real-Life Stories of Supernatural Events.* Minneapolis: Bethany House, 2012.

*Garlow, James L., and Keith Wall. *Heaven and the Afterlife.* Minneapolis: Bethany House, 2009.

*———. *Encountering Heaven and the Afterlife.* Minneapolis: Bethany House, 2010.

**Morse, Melvin. *Closer to the Light: Learning from the Near-Death Experiences of Children.* New York: Ivy, 1990.
      This is a special book.

Sabom, Michael. *Light and Death: One Doctor's Fascinating Account of Near-Death Experiences.* Grand Rapids: Zondervan, 1998.

INDIVIDUAL BIOGRAPHIES OF NDE STORIES

Note: These books tell the story of an individual's life, including their near-death experience and how it changed their life.

Alexander, Eben. *Proof of Heaven: A Neurosurgeon's Journey into the Afterlife*. New York: Simon & Schuster, 2012.

> This was a bestseller that provided very strong evidence of the afterlife. Unfortunately, many of the interpretations Alexander gives to his experience are contrary to biblical teaching. Still, it is a good read.

*Anderson, Reggie. *Appointments with Heaven: The True Story of a Country Doctor's Healing Encounters with the Hereafter*. Carol Stream, IL: Tyndale House: 2013.

> This may be the most moving book Hope and I read in this area. Incredible!

Besteman, Marvin. *My Journey to Heaven: What I Saw and How It Changed My Life*. Grand Rapids: Revell, 2012.

*Burpo, Todd. *Heaven Is for Real: A Little Boy's Astounding Story of His Trip to Heaven and Back*. With Lynn Vincent. Nashville: Nelson, 2010.

McVea, Crystal, and Alex Tresniowski. *Waking Up in Heaven: A True Story of Heaven, Brokenness, and Life Again*. New York: Howard, 2013.

*Neal, Mary C. *To Heaven and Back: A Doctor's Extraordinary Account of Her Death, Angels, and Life Again*. Colorado Springs: WaterBrook, 2011.

*Storm, Howard. *My Descent into Death: A Second Chance at Life*. New York: Doubleday, 2005.

> By his own admission, Storm was an arrogant, narcissistic, atheistic university professor who, while taking students on a trip to Paris, died and experienced demons taking him to hell. He had no idea what to do,

so he starting singing American hymns such as "God Bless America." He finally called out to Jesus, and Jesus rescued him and sent him back to earth. Storm immediately left his university post, went to seminary, and has been a pastor ever since!

COMPENDIA OF MIRACLE STORIES, ANSWERS TO PRAYER, ANGELIC ENCOUNTERS, AND NDEs

Notes: These books are deeply inspiring and really strengthen one's faith.

Canfield, Jack, Mark Victor Hansen, and LeAnn Thieman. *Chicken Soup for the Soul: A Book of Miracles.* Cos Cob, CT: Chicken Soup for the Soul Publishing, 2010.

Canfield, Jack, Mark Victor Hansen, and Amy Newmark. *Chicken Soup for the Soul: Miracles Happen.* Cos Cob, CT: Chicken Soup for the Soul Publishing, 2014.

**Crandall, Chauncey. *Touching Heaven: A Cardiologist's Encounter with Death and Living Proof of an Afterlife.* New York: FaithWords, 2015.

> This book will change your life. It is a must-read, along with John Burke's *Imagine Heaven.*

*Garlow, James, and Keith Wall. *Miracles Are for Real: What Happens When Heaven Touches Earth.* Minneapolis: Bethany House, 2011.

> Next to Crandall's *Touching Heaven*, this is Hope and my favorite.

*Garlow, James, and Keith Wall. *Real Life, Real Miracles:*

True Stories That Will Help You Believe. Minneapolis: Bethany House, 2012.

This book is also excellent and faith building.

*Shockey, Peter. *Reflections of Heaven: A Millennial Odyssey of Miracles, Angels, and Afterlife*. New York: Doubleday, 1999.

A credible book with well-supported cases of miracles, angelic encounters, and near-death experiences.

NOTES

Introduction: My Descent(s) into An Abyss of Anxiety/Depression

1. See Deborah R. Glasofer, "Am I Anxious, Depressed, or Both?" Verywell Mind, www.verywell.com/am-i-anxious -4045683?utm_campaign=list_stress&utm_medium =email&utm_source=cn_nl&utm_content=10253598& utm_term=.

CHAPTER 1: *Human Persons and a Holistic Approach for Defeating Anxiety/Depression*

1. John F. MacArthur Jr., *Our Sufficiency in Christ* (Dallas, TX: Word, 1991), 58.
2. John Wesley, *A Plain Account of Christian Perfection* (London: Epworth, 1952), 87.
3. Cf. Dallas Willard, *Renovation of the Heart* (Colorado Springs: NavPress, 2002), 27.
4. I cannot defend these claims here. For such a defense, see J. P. Moreland, *The Soul: How We Know It's Real and Why It Matters* (Chicago: Moody, 2014); Stewart Goetz and Charles Taliaferro, *A Brief History of the Soul* (Malden, MA: Wiley-Blackwell, 2011).
5. Biblical anthropological terms (*heart, soul, spirit, mind*) have a wide range of different meanings, and no specific use of a biblical term should be read into every occasion of the term. I am focusing here on a narrower, specific use of the term *spirit*.

6. See Jeffrey M. Schwartz and Rebecca Gladding, *You Are Not Your Brain: The 4-Step Solution for Changing Bad Habits, Ending Unhealthy Thinking, and Taking Control of Your Life* (New York: Penguin, 2011); Doc Childre and Deborah Rozman, *Transforming Stress: The HeartMath Solution for Relieving Worry, Fatigue, and Tension* (Oakland, CA: New Harbinger, 2005).

7. For a useful discussion of *body* and *flesh*, see G. E. Ladd, *A Theology of the New Testament* (Grand Rapids: Eerdmans, 1974), 464–75. *Flesh* may actually refer on occasion to a fleshly community, one that walks according to a legalistic adherence to the old covenant. But even in these cases of the corporate use of *flesh*, the term *sarx* is derivative of the ethical usage in reference to individuals.

8. See J. P. Moreland, "A Christian Perspective on the Impact of Modern Science on Philosophy of Mind," *Perspectives on Science and Christian Faith* 55 (March 2003): 2–12. It is important to note that Dallas Willard thought the same thing (see www.dwillard.org/articles/artview.asp?artID=117).

CHAPTER 2: *Getting a Handle on Anxiety/Depression*

1. See Edmund Bourne and Lorna Garano, *Coping with Anxiety* (Oakland, CA: New Harbinger, 2003), vii.

2. See Edmund J. Bourne, *The Anxiety & Phobia Workbook*, 5th ed. (Oakland, CA: New Harbinger, 2010), 1–4; Sean P. Egen, "Eight Facts about Anxiety and Anxiety Disorders," www.elementsbehavioralhealth.com/mental-health/8-facts-anxiety-anxiety-disorders.

3. Joseph Mercola, "Anxiety Overtakes Depression as No. 1 Mental Health Problem," June 29, 2017, http://articles.mercola.com/sites/articles/archive/2017/06/29/anxiety-overtakes-depression.aspx.

4. Kristen Neff, *Self-Compassion: The Proven Power of Being Kind to Yourself* (New York: HarperCollins, 2011), 62.

5. See Jeffrey M. Schwartz and Rebecca Gladding, *You Are Not Your Brain* (New York: Penguin, 2011), 39–45.

6. See Bourne, *Anxiety & Phobia Workbook*, 5th ed., 5–32.

7. See Bourne and Garano, *Coping with Anxiety*, 6–10; Charles Elliot and Laura Smith, *Overcoming Anxiety for Dummies* (Hoboken, NJ: Wiley, 2003), 47–50. For the most comprehensive exposition of causes of anxiety, see Bourne, *Anxiety & Phobia Workbook*, 5th ed., chapter 2.

8. I owe these insights to my good friend Dr. Bill Roth in the department of psychiatry at Loma Linda University.

9. Sonja Lyubomirsky, *The How of Happiness: A Scientific Approach to Getting the Life You Want* (New York: Penguin, 2008), 20–21.

10. Neff, *Self-Compassion*, 6.

11. In my opinion, compassion is only a part of love. Love is bigger than and goes beyond compassion. But I will use the two interchangeably. No harm will be done, and it will simplify the chapter.

12. Marina Krakovsky, "The Self-Compassion Solution," *Scientific American Mind* (May/June 2017), 66, http://the introvertentrepreneur.com/wp-content/uploads/2014/01/Self-Compassion.pdf. I owe this reference to Bill Roth.

13. Krakovsky, "Self-Compassion Solution," 68.

14. Neff, *Self-Compassion*, 8, emphasis original.

15. See Neff, *Self-Compassion*, 67–68.

16. See Adrian van Kaam, *Spirituality and the Gentle Life* (Denville, NJ: Dimension, 1974), 16.

CHAPTER 3: *Spiritual and Psychological Tools for Defeating Anxiety/Depression: Part 1*

1. Alex Williams, "Prozac Nation Is Now the United States of Xanax," *New York Times*, June 10, 2017, www.nytimes.com/

2017/06/10/style/anxiety-is-the-new-depression-xanax.
html. For the record, I believe Xanax can be a very helpful
tool for managing anxiety, a real gift from God, under the
care of a physician.

2. Dallas Willard, *Renovation of the Heart: Putting On the
Character of Christ* (Colorado Springs: NavPress, 2002), 138.

3. Edmund Bourne and Lorna Garano, *Coping with Anxiety*
(Oakland, CA: New Harbinger, 2003), 44, emphasis original.

4. Jeffrey M. Schwartz and Rebecca Gladding, *You Are Not
Your Brain: The 4-Step Solution* (New York: Avery, 2011).

5. See Harriet B. Braiker, "The Power of Self-Talk," *Psychology
Today* 23, no 12 (December 1989): 23–27. Braiker adapted
her list from David D. Burns, *The Feeling Good Handbook*
(New York: Morrow, 1989).

6. Willard, *Renovation of the Heart*, 118.

7. Don Joseph Goewey, "85 Percent of What We Worry
about Never Happens," *HuffPost*, August 25, 2016, www
.huffingtonpost.com/don-joseph-goewey-/85-of-what-we
-worry-about_b_8028368.html.

8. Many of the thoughts in this section come from J. P.
Moreland and Klaus Issler, *The Lost Virtue of Happiness*
(Colorado Springs: NavPress, 2006), 165–71.

9. See Doc Childre and Howard Martin, *The HeartMath
Solution* (San Francisco: HarperOne, 2000), chapter 1;
see also Doc Childre and Deborah Rozman, *Transforming
Stress: The HeartMath Solution for Relieving Worry,
Fatigue, and Tension* (Oakland, CA: New Harbinger, 2005).

10. C. S. Lewis, *The Abolition of Man* (New York: Macmillan,
1947), 16.

11. Childre and Martin, *HeartMath Solution*, 71, emphasis
original.

12. Childre and Martin, *HeartMath Solution*, 68–71.

13. I owe these insights to personal email correspondence with Becky Heatley, September 25, 2018.

14. Childre and Rozman, *Transforming Stress*, 83.

15. See Childre and Rozman, *Transforming Stress*, 41.

CHAPTER 4: *Spiritual and Psychological Tools for Defeating Anxiety/Depression: Part 2*

1. Personal conversation with William Roth and Susan Muto, The Epiphany Association, Pittsburgh, PA, 2014.

2. See Thomas Keating, *Open Mind, Open Heart* (New York: Continuum, 2008). Some distinguish between centering prayer and contemplative prayer, but the distinction is not important for our purposes. I will use the term *contemplative prayer* in what follows. Also, some experts in spiritual formation claim that Keating's earlier writings are solid (including the one just cited), but later in his journey he became more and more Buddhist in his orientation. Thus, some urge readers to be very discerning if they choose to read one of Keating's later books.

3. Rob Moll, *What Your Body Knows about God* (Downers Grove, IL: InterVarsity, 2014), 15.

4. Patrick J. Kiger, "The State of Sleep Deprivation in America," *National Geographic*, November 17, 2014, http://channel.nationalgeographic.com/sleepless-in-america/articles/the-state-of-sleep-deprivation-in-america.

5. Robert A. Emmons, *Gratitude Works! A 21-Day Program for Creating Emotional Prosperity* (San Francisco: Jossey-Bass, 2013), 9; see also Robert A. Emmons, *Thanks! How Practicing Gratitude Can Make You Happier* (Boston: Houghton Mifflin, 2007).

6. Emmons, *Gratitude Works!* 10.

7. See Emmons, *Gratitude Works!* 15–16.

CHAPTER 5: *Brain and Heart Tools for Defeating Anxiety/Depression*

1. See Daniel G. Amen and Lisa C. Routh, *Healing Anxiety and Depression* (New York: Penguin, 2003), 111–57; Edmund J. Bourne, *The Anxiety & Phobia Workbook*, 5th ed. (Oakland, CA: New Harbinger, 2010), 400–420. See also the sources in the annotated bibliography at the end of this book that focus on describing specific medications.

2. "How Does EMDR Work?" EMDR International Association, https://emdria.site-ym.com/?119.

3. Laurel Parnell, *Tapping In: A Step-by-Step Guide to Activating Your Healing Resources through Bilateral Stimulation* (Boulder, CO: Sounds True, 2008). Please note the extensive disclaimer on the copyright page of Parnell's book. I affirm this same disclaimer.

4. Parnell, *Tapping In*, 45–76.

5. Doc Childre and Deborah Rozman, *Transforming Stress: The HeartMath Solution for Relieving Worry, Fatigue, and Tension* (Oakland, CA: New Harbinger, 2005), 1. I have gleaned most of the information in this section from this excellent book.

6. See Childre and Rozman, *Transforming Stress*, 66.

7. Childre and Rozman, *Transforming Stress*, 19.

8. Childre and Rozman, *Transforming Stress*, 6.

9. Childre and Rozman, *Transforming Stress*, 101.

10. See Childre and Rozman, *Transforming Stress*, 36.

11. See Childre and Rozman, *Transforming Stress*, 14; see their discussion on pp. 13–18.

12. Childre and Rozman, *Transforming Stress*, 31.

13. See Childre and Rozman, *Transforming Stress*, 43–47.

14. See Childre and Rozman, *Transforming Stress*, 75.

Chapter 6: *Suffering, Healing, and Disappointment with God*

1. Daniel Amen and Lisa Routh, *Healing Anxiety and Depression* (New York: Penguin, 2003), 184.
2. Edmund Bourne and Lorna Garano, *Coping with Anxiety* (Oakland, CA: New Harbinger, 2003,) 44, emphasis original.
3. Christopher Lasch, *The Culture of Narcissism: American Life in an Age of Diminished Expectations* (New York: Norton, 1979), 42; see his discussion on pp. 42–51.
4. Lasch, *Culture of Narcissism*, 51.
5. Roger Cohen, "Secular Europe's Merits," *New York Times*, December 13, 2007, www.nytimes.com/2007/12/13/opinion/13cohen.html.
6. Dallas Willard, *The Divine Conspiracy* (San Francisco: HarperSanFrancisco, 1998), 92; see pp. 75, 79, 134, 184–85.
7. Edmund J. Bourne, *The Anxiety & Phobia Workbook*, 5th ed. (Oakland, CA: New Harbinger, 2010), 448.
8. Bourne, *Anxiety & Phobia Workbook*, 5th ed., 449, emphasis added.
9. C. S. Lewis, *A Grief Observed* (1961; repr., New York: HarperCollins, 1994), 5–6.
10. See Francis MacNutt, *Healing* (Notre Dame, IN: Ave Maria, 1999), 61–70; see also the still relevant book by Jack Deere, *Surprised by the Power of the Spirit* (Grand Rapids: Zondervan, 1993).
11. MacNutt, *Healing*, 61, emphasis original.
12. Francis MacNutt, *The Healing Reawakening: Reclaiming Our Lost Inheritance* (Grand Rapids: Chosen, 2005), 105, emphasis original.
13. For an excellent resource on gaining a biblical perspective on suffering, see Timothy Keller, *Walking with God through Pain and Suffering* (New York: Dutton, 2013).
14. Larry Crabb, *Shattered Dreams: God's Unexpected Path to Joy* (Colorado Springs: WaterBrook, 2001), 30.

220 · FINDING QUIET

15. Crabb, *Shattered Dreams*, 31, emphasis original. For more
on this topic, see Philip Yancey, *Disappointment with God*
(Grand Rapids: Zondervan, 1988); *Where Is God When It
Hurts?* (Grand Rapids: Zondervan, 1990).
16. For helpful resources on lament prayers in the Bible, see
Dan B. Allender and Tremper Longman III, *The Cry of
the Soul: How Our Emotions Reveal Our Deepest Questions
about God* (Colorado Springs: NavPress, 1994); Bernhard
W. Anderson, *Out of the Depths: The Psalms Speak for Us
Today* (New York: United Methodist Church, 1970); Walter
Brueggemann, *The Message of the Psalms* (Minneapolis:
Fortress, 1984); Walter Bruggemann, *Spirituality of the
Psalms* (Minneapolis: Fortress, 2002); Ingvar Fløysvik,
*When God Becomes My Enemy: The Theology of the
Complaint Psalms* (St. Louis, MO: Concordia, 1997);
Tremper Longman III, *How to Read the Psalms* (Downers
Grove, IL: InterVarsity, 1988).